D1007169

598

30

SCRIPTS

FOR

RELAXATION
IMAGERY
& INNER HEALING

VOLUME 2

30

SCRIPTS

FOR

RELAXATION
IMAGERY
& INNER HEALING

VOLUME 2

Edited by

Julie T. Lusk

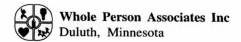

Whole Person Associates Inc
Duluth, Minnesota

Whole Person Associates Inc
210 West Michigan
Duluth MN 55802-1908
218-727-0500

30 Scripts for Relaxation, Imagery & Inner Healing, Volume 2

Printed in the United States of America by Versa Press

10 9 8 7 6 5 4 3

Publisher: Donald A Tubesing
Editorial Director: Susan Gustafson
Manuscript Editor: Patrick Gross
Art Director: Joy Morgan Dey

Library of Congress Cataloging-in-Publication Data
(Revised for vol. 2)

30 scripts for relaxation, imagery & inner healing.

    1. Relaxation.   2. Stress management.   3. Imagery
(Psychology)—Therapeutic use.   I. Lusk, Julie T.
II. Title: Thirty scripts for relaxation, imagery &
inner healing.
RA785.A14   1992   129   92-80231
ISBN 0-938586-69-6 (v. 1 : pbk.)
ISBN 0-938586-76-9 (v. 2 : pbk.)

To

Dave, my husband,
for your love, helpfulness,
and sense of humor

Angie, my Mom,
for your friendship and encouragement

My family,
especially Tom Tapin, the Lusks' and Nichols'

Sallie Garst and Judy Fulop,
for your kindness and support

All those who contributed a script to 30 Scripts.
Without your generosity and cooperation
these books would not have been possible

My yoga students and counseling clients,
for inspiring me

And to
The entire staff at Whole Person Associates

Contents

Foreword

Welcome to the second volume of *30 Scripts for Relaxation, Imagery & Inner Healing*. This volume, like the first, contains relaxation and imagery scripts that focus on relaxing the body and mind, connecting with nature, discovering and learning from wise inner guides, healing physical and emotional injuries, and discovering more about yourself. I also included a cross-reference index, which organizes the scripts from both volumes into specific categories, such as enhancing intuition, strengthening self-esteem, and making behavioral changes.

Taking time to think, daydream, and relax is rarely valued in today's society. We live in a time of information overload. We try to do so much so fast that even waiting a couple seconds is waiting too long. The guided meditations and imageries in both volumes of *30 Scripts* will help you explore and develop your internal life of thought, emotion, and spirit. It's well worth the effort.

Independently and in collaboration, knowledgeable people from the fields of medicine, biology, physics, religion, and psychology are concluding that the mind/body/spirit connection holds incredible power and promise for health and happiness. This important connection comes alive through the exercises in *30 Scripts*.

As always, feel free to use the scripts as they are written, or to change them in any way you like, or to add your own ideas. Whatever you do, use your imagination and be creative.

This book is meant to be *experienced*. Read it to someone or have someone read it to you. Only then will these exercises become truly vibrant, meaningful, and rewarding.

Julie Tapin Lusk
February 1993

Series Introduction

Many group leaders are aware of the benefits of guided imagery but have had little experience in the field. Here are some tips to help you use these scripts effectively.

Working with guided meditations

Everyone is different, so each participant will experience guided imagery uniquely. These individual differences should be encouraged. During a guided meditation, some people will imagine vivid scenes, colors, images, or sounds while others will focus on what they are feeling. This is why a combination of sights, sounds, and feelings have been incorporated into the scripts. With practice, it is possible to expand your participants' range of awareness.

By careful selection of images you can help deepen their experience and cultivate their awareness in new areas that can enrich their lives. For instance, people who are most comfortable in the visual area can be encouraged to stretch their awareness and increase their sensitivity to feelings and sounds.

Working with guided imagery is powerful and it is up to you to use this book responsibly and ethically. Leaders with little or no training in guided imagery may use these scripts with emotionally healthy people. Be careful, however, when presenting themes and techniques that are unfamiliar to you. Since people respond in a variety of ways to visualization, avoid generalizing about the benefits of any given script.

If your groups are composed of people who are emotionally ill or especially fragile, you should seek out special training or professional guidance before introducing them to visualizations.

Preparing the group or individual

Physical relaxation reduces anxiety, activates the creative right brain, and enhances the ability to concentrate on mental images. Some type of physical relaxation sequence should be used prior to any guided meditation. You'll find a variety of relaxation exercises to choose from in section one of both volumes.

Breathing properly is essential for complete and total relaxation. Unfortunately, very few people take full breaths, especially when under stress. When a person consciously takes deep breaths, stress is reduced and the mind can remain calm and in control. It is important that people focus on their breathing, taking in full deep breaths through the nose.

Before beginning any guided meditation, briefly describe the images you will use and ask if they make anyone feel uncomfortable. People who are afraid of water may find images of ocean waves to be frightening rather than calming. Be prepared with an alternate image. Let participants know that if they become uncomfortable, they may, at any time, open their eyes and tune out the visualization.

As you read a script, people will follow you for a while and then drift off into their own imaginations. They will usually tune you back in later on. If they know this in advance, they won't feel as if they are failing by being inattentive. So tell them this is normal and to let it happen.

Choosing the right atmosphere

Select a room that has comfortable chairs for sitting or a carpeted floor for lying down. Close the door and shut the windows to block out distracting noises.

If possible, dim the lights to create a relaxing environment. Low lights enhance the ability to relax by blocking out visual distractions. If the room lights cannot be controlled to your satisfaction, bring along a lamp or a night light.

Adjust the thermostat so that the room temperature is warm and comfortable. If the room is too cool, it will be hard to relax and remain focused. Suggest that people wear a sweater or jacket if they think they may get cold.

If distractions occur—a noisy air conditioner, traffic, loud conversations—try raising your voice, using shorter phrases and fewer pauses, or incorporating the sounds into the guided meditation. For example, you might say, "Notice how the humming sounds of the air conditioner relax you more and more," or "If your mind begins to drift, gently bring it back to the sound of my voice."

Using your voice

Speak in a calm, comforting, and steady manner. Let your voice flow. Your voice should be smooth and somewhat monotonous. But don't whisper.

Start with your voice at a volume that can be easily heard. As the guided meditation progresses and as the participants' awareness increases, you may begin speaking more softly. As a person relaxes, hearing acuity increases. Bring your voice up when suggesting tension and bring it down when suggesting relaxation. Near the end of the guided meditation, return to using an easily heard volume. This will help participants come back.

You may tell participants to use a hand signal if they cannot hear you. Advise people with hearing impairments to sit close to you.

Pacing yourself

Read the guided meditations slowly, but not so slowly that you lose people. Begin at a conversational pace and slow down as the relaxation progresses. It's easy to go too fast, so take your time. Don't rush.

The ellipses used throughout the book indicate a brief pause. Spaces between paragraphs signal a longer pause.

Leader's notes and script divisions are printed in italics and should not be read out loud.

Give participants time to follow your instructions. If you suggest that they wiggle their toes, watch them do so, then wait for them to stop wiggling their toes before going on. When your participants are relaxed and engaged in the imagery process, they have tapped into their subconscious (slow, rich, imagery) mind—and they shouldn't be hurried.

When you're leading the meditation, you're still in your conscious (alert and efficient) mind. Pay careful attention to all participants. You may have to repeat an instruction if you see that people are not following you.

To help you with your volume and tone, pace and timing, listen to a tape of yourself leading guided meditations.

As you reach the end of a meditation, help participants make the transition back to the present. Tell them to visualize their surroundings, to stretch, and to breathe deeply. Repeat these instructions until everyone is alert.

Using music

Using music to enhance relaxation is not a new idea. History is full of examples of medicine men and women, philosophers, priests, scientists, and musicians who used music to heal. In fact, music seems to be an avenue of communication for some people where no other avenues appear to exist.

Your music should be cued up and ready to go at the right volume before you start your meditation. Nothing ruins the atmosphere more quickly than having the leader fool around trying to get the audio tape going.

Jim Borling, a board certified music therapist, makes the following suggestions on selecting music.

Tips on Music Selection

- Custom select music for individual clients or classes whenever possible. Not everyone responds in a similar fashion to the same music.

- Matching a person's present emotional state with music is known as the ISO principle. If you can match the initial state and then gradually begin changing the music, the person's emotional state will change along with the music. If a person is agitated or angry, begin with fast-paced music, then change to slower-paced selections as relaxation deepens.

- Choose music that has flowing melodies rather than disjointed and fragmented melodies.

- Don't assume that the type of music you find relaxing will be relaxing to others. Have a variety of musical styles available and ask your clients for suggestions.

- Try using sounds from nature like ocean waves. Experiment with New Age music and Space music, much of which is appropriate for relaxation work. Classical music may be effective, especially movements that are marked *largo* or *adagio*.

- Adjust the volume so that it doesn't drown out your voice. On the other hand, music that is too soft may cause your listeners to strain to hear it.

- Select music based upon the mood desired. Sedative music is soothing and produces a contemplative mood. Stimulative music increases bodily energy and stimulates the emotions.

- Select music with a slow tempo and low pitch. The higher the pitch or frequency of sound, the more likely it will be irritating.

Musical Recommendations

New Age: *Comfort Zone, Spectrum Suite, Effortless Relaxation* by Steven Halpern. 800-247-6789. *Listen to the Peace I, II* by Diane and Terrill Jones. 703/929-4183. *The Fairy Ring, The Brighter Side, Solace* by Mike Rowland. 414/272-1199. Also try samplers from Windham Hill, Narada, and Hearts of Space.

Classical: *Relax with the Classics* by Lind Institute. 800-462-3766. Meditation: *Classical Relaxation*, Delta Music, Inc. 213-826-6151.

Nature and Environments: *Interludes: Soothing Sounds of Nature and Music,* Great American Audio Corp., 33 Portman Rd., New Rochelle, NY 10801. Environmental Sounds: *Ocean, Sailing, English Meadow, Crickets,* Syntonic Research, 175 Fifth Ave. NY, NY 10010.

Processing the experience

You may wish to add to the richness of the guided meditations by asking participants afterwards to share their experiences with others. This can be facilitated by creating an atmosphere of trust. Ask the group open-ended questions that relate to the theme of the exercise. Be accepting and empathetic towards everyone. Respect everyone's comments and never be judgmental or critical, even if people express negative reactions.

Caution

Do not force people to participate in anything that may be uncomfortable for them. Give ample permission to everyone to only do things that feel safe. Tell them that if an image seems threatening, they can change it to something that feels right or they can stop the imaging process, stretch, and open their eyes. Emphasize to participants that they are in total control and are able to leave their image-filled subconscious mind and return to their alert, rational conscious mind at any time they choose.

Advise participants that it is not safe to practice meditation or visualization while driving or operating machinery.

The relaxation scripts, guided meditations, and creative visualizations in this book are not intended to provide or be a substitute for medical or psychological advice on personal health matters. If this assistance is needed, consult a physician, therapist, or other health care professional. Neither the editor, contributors, nor Whole Person Associates assumes responsibility for the improper use of the relaxation scripts, guided meditations, and creative visualizations contained in this book.

Taping the scripts

You may audiotape the scripts for your own personal or professional use. You may not, however, copy or distribute the scripts to others on audiotape or in written form.

SECTION ONE Becoming Relaxed

The cornerstone of all guided imagery work lies in the ability to relax the body, mind, and emotions. This is true whether you would like to awaken your intuition, communicate with your inner guide, connect with nature, or benefit from the healing visualizations. You will be wasting your time if you don't relax first.

Practice the following exercises until you become comfortable doing them. The method used for relaxing isn't important; being able to relax is. Relaxation opens the door to your inner resources. Try out each exercise several times and choose the ones that work best for you.

After you've mastered the relaxation exercises, explore the different types of guided visualizations in the other sections of this book, or of those from volume 1.

Relaxing while Lying Down

Julie T. Lusk

Time: 10 minutes

Participants lie down and relax by alternately tensing and relaxing all muscle groups and by mentally releasing tension.

Script

Begin by closing your eyes.

Draw your attention to your right leg . . . Tense it and feel it from your toes to your thigh and hip, tighter and tighter . . . Now release, letting all the tension and tightness drain from your leg . . . Feel the relaxation in your leg.

Shift your attention to your left leg . . . Tense it and feel it from your toes to your thigh. Know it, hold it, feel the energy and heat . . . Now relax.

Roll your legs gently back and forth and let them rest. Become fully aware of the different way tension and relaxation feel in your legs.

Your feet are relaxed . . . your ankles are relaxed . . . your calves . . . knees . . . thighs . . .

and hips are relaxed. Let your legs feel
completely supported by the ground. Notice
if they feel warm and comfortable . . . sinking
into the ground . . . feeling heavier and heavier.
Resolve to let your legs stay still.

Draw your attention to your fanny. Tense
the muscles in your fanny, hold, tighter and
tighter . . . And relax, allowing the muscles to
let go.

Focus your attention on your abdominal area.
Pull your muscles in . . . Now relax . . . Feel the
knots untie.

This time, push your abdominal muscles out
and tense and hold them . . . Now let go. You
feel calm and relaxed . . . peaceful and serene,
feeling better and better.

Take in a nice, full breath, letting the air come all
the way in so that your abdomen raises up . . .
Now let the air out, feeling more and more
relaxed, full of peace and contentment.

Shift your attention to your right arm. Tense
it completely, from your hands up to your
shoulders. Tighter and tighter, feeling the power
and energy . . . And relax, releasing entirely.

Let your arm feel completely supported by the

floor. Feel your arm get heavier and heavier as it relaxes more and more.

Draw your attention to your left arm. Tighten up the muscles from your hands all the way up to your shoulders, more and more . . . Now relax, letting all the tension go.

You may gently roll your arms from side to side . . . and then let them come to rest. Your fingers are relaxed, your hands are relaxed, your wrists, lower arms, elbows, upper arms, and shoulders are all relaxed, completely relaxed.

Allow your arms to feel like they are sinking into the floor. Feeling comfortable and at ease, resolve to let your arms stay still.

Focus your attention on your face. Even though your eyes are already closed, squint your eyes and tense your eyes and eyelids . . . Now relax. Tighten up your nose and cheeks and lips . . . Now let go. Let each and every muscle relax and smooth out.

To relax your mouth and jaw, press your lips together. Feel the tightness . . . Now relax. Press your tongue against the roof of your mouth and hold . . . Now let go completely.

This time, open up your mouth and move your jaw up and down and back and forth, fast and slow, working out all of the tension . . . Now relax, letting your lips part slightly.

Your tongue is at rest and suspended in your mouth . . . your lips are parted . . . and your jaw is loose.

To relax even more, mentally scan your body, letting everything relax more and more.

Your feet are relaxed . . . your calves are relaxed . . . your knees are relaxed . . . your thighs . . . your fanny and pelvis are relaxed . . . your lower back . . . mid-back . . . upper back and shoulders are all relaxed.

Allow your upper arms . . . your elbows . . . your forearms . . . your hands and your fingers to relax. All are relaxed.

Feel your torso and the organs in your abdomen relaxing completely . . . And now your lungs . . . Feel your neck relax and all the muscles in your face relax. Your mouth . . . cheeks . . . nose . . . eyes, and forehead are relaxed. The top of your head, the back of your head, and all the way down to your toes.

Feel yourself become more and more relaxed. Each time you exhale, notice how much more you can relax, deeper and deeper.

If you would be more comfortable, you may put your feet on the floor with your knees bent, or you may stay just as you are. You are feeling peaceful and calm, perfectly safe and serene. Notice how your body is feeling right here, right now. Memorize this feeling, let it sink in. Know that it can be created anytime you wish.

Pause

Continue with a visualization exercise or say the following:

Now bring your attention back to the room. Feel the floor underneath you . . . Picture the walls, ceiling, and floor.

I am going to count from five to one. As I count, you will progressively begin feeling alert and alive. 5 . . . 4 . . . 3 . . . 2 . . . and 1. Begin to stretch and move. Open your eyes, feeling relaxed, peaceful, and alert.

Repeat the above instructions until everyone is alert.

Expanding and Contracting

Julie T. Lusk

Time: 4 minutes

This short relaxation exercise, performed while lying down, combines progressive relaxation with breathing and body scanning techniques.

Script

Lie down on the floor and close your eyes. Become aware of your body. All at once, stretch out and tense your arms and legs, open your eyes up wide, spread out your fingers and toes, stretch out your tongue, and raise your body a few inches from the floor. Hold . . . Now relax. Let your body go loose.

Now contract and pull in. Pull your feet in, compress your abdomen, make a fist, squint your eyes, and purse your lips and nose. Hold . . . Now let go. Relax.

Take in a full, deep breath and fill up the lower part of your lungs so that your abdomen raises up . . . Open your mouth and let the air rush out.

Take in another full, deep breath and fill up the mid and upper portion of your lungs. Feel your rib cage expanding . . . Open your mouth and let the air rush out.

Let your breath return to normal . . . Each time you breathe out, you relax more and more.

You can relax even more if you let your mind scan your body and give yourself mental permission to relax even more.

Your feet are relaxed . . . your calves are relaxed . . . your knees are relaxed . . . your thighs and your fanny are relaxed . . . your lower back . . . mid-back . . . upper back, and shoulders are all relaxed.

Allow your upper arms . . . your elbows . . . your forearms . . . your hands, and your fingers to relax. All are relaxed. Feel your torso and the organs in your abdomen relaxing completely . . . And now your lungs.

Feel your neck relax and all the muscles in your face relax. Your mouth . . . cheeks . . . nose . . . eyes, and forehead are relaxed. The feeling of relaxation spreads from the top of your head to the back of your head and all the way down to your toes. Feel yourself become more and more relaxed.

Pause

Continue with a visualization exercise or say the following:

When you are ready, gently begin to stretch and move about. Open your eyes, feeling calm and relaxed.

Repeat the above instructions until everyone is alert.

Magic Carpet Ride

Judy Fulop

Time: 15 minutes

This deep breathing exercise works well for people who have difficulty with relaxed breathing.

Script

Get into a comfortable position, close your eyes, and pretend that you are on a magic carpet . . . Let yourself picture your magic carpet. Is it orange, green, blue, or some other color? Does it have designs? What does it feel like when you touch it? Is it soft?

Now imagine lying on the magic carpet in a safe place . . . This could be your favorite place, your room, somewhere outdoors, some place inside, or any other place you choose. If you want, you can even create your own fantasy place . . . Just imagine a place that is safe and comfortable.

As you take in your next deep breath, allow your feet to tighten into a ball . . . Then let your breath out as you allow your feet to relax.

Do this once more . . . Take in a deep breath and

tighten your feet . . . then let the air out and
relax your feet, as if you were letting your feet
melt into jelly.

Now move up to your legs. Tighten the muscles
in your legs while you take another breath . . .
and let them relax when you let the air out.

Move to your hips and do the same thing. Take
in a deep breath as you tense up your hips . . .
Now release the tightness in your hips as you
let your breath go.

This time, take in a nice deep breath while you
tighten up your stomach muscles . . . Now let
your breath out as you soften your stomach
muscles.

Push your shoulders up to your ears as you
bring in a breath. Now let go of your shoulders
and your breath at the same time . . . Good.

OK, bring your attention to your arms and
hands. Tighten up your arms and make two fists
as you breathe in. Hold for a second . . . and
now let go of the tightness in your arms and
hands while you let your breath go.

Lastly, make a jack-o'-lantern face by tightening
all the muscles in your face . . . And now relax
your face as much as you can. Let your mouth
open a little bit, and let the rest of your face
soften from your forehead to your chin.

Now take in a deep breath and tighten up your entire body . . . from your toes, knees, hips, on up to your arms and face . . . then let all your muscles relax while you let the air out.

As you relax, feel your body sinking into your magic carpet. Just let it support you. If you wish, allow the magic carpet to slowly and gently move up and rest on a cushion of air.

Pause for 30 seconds

As you relax on your magic carpet, take a deep breath, allowing your belly to rise . . . and then your chest to rise . . . When you let the air out, let your belly and chest sink down into the magic carpet.

Let your breath flow in and out. Effortless and easy . . . slow and easy. As you breathe, see or feel the air moving into your chest and going down your trachea, the tube leading to your lungs. If you can, breathe through your nose. If not, breathe through your mouth . . . Slow and smooth.

As the air moves down your trachea, allow your whole body to relax. When you are relaxed, the muscles around the trachea will relax . . . and as these muscles relax, the trachea will become larger so that it can take in more oxygen-rich air. Just see or feel these muscles expanding and relaxing.

Feel or see the air going into your lungs, where it then divides into more tubes, like branches on a tree, taking the nourishing air to the innermost parts of your lungs.

Imagine that the tubes are open wide to let the air in and out . . . As the air continues through your lungs, it passes through tubes that divide into smaller sacs, which look like grapes. These sacs open up to allow in more oxygen-rich air. Blood vessels, which surround the sacs, pick up oxygen from the air and take it to other places in your body.

Thank the sacs for getting oxygen to your blood and, thereby, to the rest of our body.

Your blood cells also give carbon dioxide back to the sacs to be carried up though the air passage-ways, into the trachea, and out with your breath.

When you breathe out, allow the air to pass out of your nose (or mouth) and out of your body. You are still relaxed, so the air moves in and out freely and easily.

Remember this relaxed feeling and allow yourself to relax this way whenever you feel your muscles begin to tense up, or if you feel a tightness in your chest.

Take in one last slow breath, allowing fresh air

to move freely all the way to your lungs. See the oxygen being exchanged for carbon dioxide, where the inner parts of the lungs meet your blood cells. Now exhale, allowing the carbon dioxide to move freely out of your lungs.

The more relaxed you feel on your magic carpet or anywhere else, the more air can move freely in and out of your lungs. You can do this relaxation when you are about to play a game, take a big test, or whenever you begin to have a problem with breathing. Just let yourself relax, whether you are in a chair, lying in your bed, or on your magic carpet.

Take in a deep breath, and as you slowly let it go relax all the muscles in your body, especially the tubes that take air in and out of your lungs. If your magic carpet is floating right now on a cushion of air, allow it to gently settle down and touch this floor.

Pause

Continue with a visualization exercise or say the following:

With your same relaxed breathing, slowly begin to open your eyes and come back into this room, taking your time, allowing your whole body to stay relaxed.

Repeat the above instructions until everyone is alert.

Threshold Relaxation

John Zach

Time: 12 minutes

In this exercise, participants slightly tense a specific part of their body until it begins to feel tense. Once tension is felt, it is held a moment and then relaxed. *Threshold Relaxation* teaches participants to be sensitive to small changes in the body. Through practice the body learns what relaxation feels like in each muscle and how to regulate itself in automatic and unconscious ways.

It takes practice for the body to become aware of tension and to release it on such a fine level and in such a defined area. When teaching your clients this script, emphasize the importance of tensing only the specific area they are concentrating on and have them practice this technique several times a day for the first couple of weeks.

Take it slow and in time your clients will be able to quickly control their relaxation response. This relaxation technique works even better when clients can imagine what it looks like as a muscle is being tensed and then relaxed. It may be helpful to have them look through a basic book on anatomy to get an accurate picture of what muscles look like.

Script

To begin, slightly tense your hands . . . hold . . . and relax . . . Remember to focus on the holding on . . . and letting go . . . Again, slightly tense your hands, to the point where you can hardly

feel any movement . . . hold . . . and relax. Notice
the difference between how it feels to have
tension and then to be relaxed.

Now focus on your forearms. Slightly tense your
forearms. Noticing the tension . . . hold . . . and
relax. Notice the difference in the sensations.

Move your awareness to your biceps. Barely
tense your biceps . . . hold . . . and relax.

Now slightly tense your shoulders . . . ever so
slightly . . . hold . . . and relax. Notice how easy
it is to be tense or relaxed.

Know that your body can become much more
relaxed.

Now slightly tense your neck muscles . . .
hold . . . and relax . . . Notice the amount of
tension you hold in this area and how easy it is
to allow these muscles to feel more relaxed.

Move to the lower facial muscles and tense just a
tiny bit . . . hold . . . and relax.

Now move to the upper face and scalp . . . tense
ever so slightly . . . hold . . . and relax.

Now take in a deep breath and notice the
muscle tension as the air goes in. Hold your
breath . . . Now let go and relax.

Breathe in . . . and out. Notice how breathing is a
natural process of holding on and letting go.

As you breathe in, notice how you tense your
chest muscles ever so slightly . . . then hold, ever
so slightly. Now relax.

Move to your back muscles . . . tense them ever
so slightly and hold . . . Now relax.

Go to your stomach area . . . tense it, notice the
tension, hold on . . . and now let go. Notice your
increased level of relaxation.

Move your awareness to your thigh muscles . . .
Tense slightly. Notice the tension . . . and relax.

Go to your calf muscles . . . tense, easy does
it . . . and relax. Now to your feet. Slightly tense
them, hold . . . and relax.

Now that you have completed tensing the
major muscle groups, go back to any muscles
that may still feel tense and adjust them in any
way you want to allow yourself to be more
relaxed and comfortable.

Pause

Continue with a visualization exercise or say the following:

Now spend a minute just enjoying this relaxed feeling. Take as much time as you like. When you are ready, allow your attention to come back to the here and now. Then stretch out and open your eyes, feeling awake and refreshed as if you had just slept a full eight hours.

Repeat the above instructions until everyone is alert.

Heavy

Don Tubesing

Time: 15 minutes

This script helps participants experience the freshness of spirit and calmness of mind that results from passive attention to the rhythm of their breathing and the relaxed heaviness in their hands and feet.

Script

Prepare yourself to relax now. Prepare yourself to experience calm . . . to feel quiet . . . to know peace. Find a comfortable position . . . Begin to sink down . . . and be supported by your surrounding environment.

Close your eyes now . . . and focus on breathing naturally. Inhale . . . and fill yourself with life-giving air. Exhale . . . and relax . . . allowing your body to sink . . . breathing in . . . and breathing out.

Begin to withdraw your thoughts from your surroundings . . . and to center your focus inward on the peace . . . and the stillness . . . within you. Prepare yourself with an attitude of passive attention . . . alert but quiet . . . aware . . . yet at peace.

And . . . making nothing happen . . . you let go of the tension of controlling anything . . . you watch the relaxation you feel spread to all parts of your being.

And you breathe in . . . easily . . . and breathe out naturally. Part of the rhythm . . . of all life.

And you focus on your breathing. As you breathe in . . . you say to yourself . . . "I am." As you breathe out . . . you say to yourself . . . "relaxed."

I am . . . relaxed.

I am . . . relaxed.

I am . . . relaxed.

I am . . . calm.

I am . . . comfortable.

I am . . . relaxed.

I am . . . relaxing . . . into the supports around me. My mind is quiet. My whole body is relaxed.

I am . . . at peace.

I notice . . . my quiet.

I notice . . . my peace.

I notice . . . my calm.

I think about my right hand . . . I allow my right
hand to become heavy with my breathing . . .
My right hand is becoming heavy . . . My right
hand is heavy . . . and relaxed.

I allow the heaviness of my hand to spread up
my arm . . . I think about my right arm . . . I
allow my right arm to become heavy with my
breathing. My right arm is becoming heavy . . .
My right arm is heavy . . . and relaxed. My right
hand and arm are heavy and relaxed.

I think about my left hand . . . I allow my left
hand to become heavy with my breathing . . .
My left hand is becoming heavy . . . My left
hand is heavy . . . and relaxed.

I allow the heaviness of my hand to spread up
my left arm . . . I think about my left arm . . . I
allow my left arm to become heavy with my
breathing . . . My left arm is becoming heavy . . .
My left arm is heavy and relaxed.

My left hand and arm are heavy and relaxed. I
think about both of my hands and arms . . . I
allow both hands and arms to become relaxed . . .
and heavy . . . with my breathing.

My hands and arms are heavy. My hands
and arms are heavy and relaxed. I continue to
breathe deeply . . . rhythmically.

I allow the heaviness of my hands and arms . . .
to spread down my back to my right leg and
foot . . . I feel the weight of my body . . . and my
back. My hands are warm and heavy . . . My
back is relaxed. My legs and feet are becoming
heavy.

Pause

I think about my right foot . . . I allow my right
foot to become heavy with my breathing . . . My
right foot is becoming heavy . . . My right foot is
heavy . . . and relaxed.

I allow the heaviness to spread to my leg . . .
I think about my right leg . . . I allow my right
leg to become heavy with my breathing . . . My
right leg is becoming heavy . . . My right leg is
heavy . . . and relaxed.

My right foot and leg are heavy and relaxed.

I allow the heaviness of my foot and leg . . . to
spread across my hips . . . and down my left leg
to my left foot.

I think about my left foot . . . I allow my left foot
to become heavy with my breathing . . . My left

foot is becoming heavy . . . My left foot is heavy . . . and relaxed.

I allow this heaviness to spread to my leg . . . I think about my left leg . . . I allow my left leg to become heavy with my breathing . . . My left leg is becoming heavy . . . My left leg is heavy . . . and relaxed.

I think about my feet and legs . . . I allow both feet and legs to become relaxed and heavy . . . My feet and my legs are becoming heavy . . . My feet and my legs are heavy . . . and relaxed.

I imagine tiny weights attached to my arms and legs . . . making my arms and legs heavy . . . gently pulling my arms and legs down . . . My arms and legs are sinking . . . relaxing.

Both of my legs are heavy. Both of my arms are heavy.

My hands and my arms are heavy . . . and relaxed. My feet and my legs are heavy . . . and relaxed.

My hands and arms . . . feet and legs . . . are heavy . . . and relaxed.

I am . . . comfortable.

I am . . . quiet.

I am . . . at ease.

My body is in tune with my mind . . .
and connected by my breathing.

I am . . . heavy.

I am . . . relaxed.

I am . . . quiet.

I feel the energy flowing . . . through my arms to
my hands . . . through my legs to my feet.

I am alive.

I am refreshed.

I am relaxed.

I feel a freshness of spirit.

Pause

Continue with a visualization exercise or say the following:

Now prepare to open your eyes. Take a deep
breath . . . and open your eyes . . . slowly . . .
while you remain fully relaxed.

Now gently stretch . . . but remain relaxed.
Begin preparing yourself to return to your
world . . . relaxed . . . and refreshed.

Your eyes are open . . . You are aware of your
surroundings . . . but you remain relaxed . . .
and calm. You prepare to move on . . . with a
calm energy.

Refreshed now . . . Renewed now . . . Relaxed
now. You take these feelings with you as you
move on with your day.

Repeat the above instructions until everyone is alert.

This and the following script are available on audiotape from
Whole Person Associates Inc.

Warm

Nancy Loving Tubesing

Time: 15 minutes

This autogenic relaxation routine asks participants to gently focus on warmth spreading through their bodies, bringing complete relaxation and a sense of personal peace and renewal.

Script

Begin to relax now . . . and to let go of the cares of your day.

Begin to expect that you will become rebalanced and reenergized . . . by the quiet and peace that you will give to yourself.

Close your eyes gently . . . and let them be still. Unfold your arms . . . and allow them to relax. Uncross your legs . . . and settle back.

You are resting comfortably . . . feeling the support beneath your body . . . and allowing your breathing to find its natural, steady, effortless rhythm.

As you allow yourself to relax more and more completely, do not try to make something happen . . . Rather, allow yourself to watch and notice your experience as it happens.

Now focus your attention on your breathing. Say in your mind . . . I am breathing . . . naturally. I am breathing . . . easily. I am breathing . . . freely . . . without restriction.

I take a deep . . . slow breath. I hold it a moment . . . then I breathe out and let go completely. I take another slow, deep breath . . . I hold it a moment . . . then let the breath go . . . easily . . . completely.

I fill myself with air . . . as I breathe in. I let go completely as I breathe out.

I am beginning to feel relaxed.

I feel the flow of my breath . . . throughout my body. As I breathe in . . . my breath fills every part of me. As I breathe out . . . all the tension flows out with my breathing.

I am comfortable.

I am relaxed.

I am quiet.

I breathe in . . . and I breathe out. I notice the

life-giving tides of my breathing. In . . . and out.
In . . . and out.

Pause 40 seconds

My thoughts are turned inward . . . and at rest.
I am at ease. Deep down in my mind I visualize
myself as completely relaxed . . . And I let go of
any leftover tension I notice.

I imagine myself lying in the gentle sun . . . It is
warm . . . and my body soaks up the warmth.

I notice that my hands are pleasantly warmed by
the sun. And I turn my palms upward . . . to let
them enjoy the sensation of warmth . . . and
soak up the sun's healing energy.

I focus on my right hand . . . It is warm. My
right hand is relaxed . . . and warm. My right
hand is relaxed . . . and warm. My right hand is
relaxed and warm.

My breathing gets deeper and deeper . . . And I
relax more and more fully.

The warmth of my right hand spreads up my
arm. My right arm is relaxed . . . and warm. My
right arm is relaxed . . . and warm.

My right shoulder and the back of my neck
receive warmth . . . from my right hand and arm.

Pause

I focus on my left hand . . . It is warm. My left hand is relaxed . . . and warm. My left hand is relaxed . . . and warm. My left hand is relaxed and warm.

My breathing gets deeper and deeper . . . and I relax more and more fully.

The warmth in my left hand spreads up my arm . . . My left arm is relaxed . . . and warm. My left arm is relaxed . . . and warm.

My left shoulder and the back of my neck receive warmth . . . from my left hand . . . and arm.

My breathing gets deeper and deeper . . . as I relax more and more fully.

My hands and my arms are relaxed and warm . . . My hands and my arms are comfortable and warm.

I breathe with my abdomen. I breathe deeply . . . And the tides of my breathing relax me.

The warmth of my breathing spreads to my legs . . . and my feet. My feet and my legs are becoming relaxed and warm.

I focus on my right foot . . . and notice that my right foot is becoming warm. My right foot is relaxed . . . and warm. My right foot is relaxed and warm.

As the warmth spreads up . . . into my hips and belly. I focus again on my steady breathing and allow the tides of my breathing to relax me . . . In and out . . . spreading warmth and relaxation to every part of my body.

I focus now on my left foot . . . and notice that my left foot is becoming warm. My left foot is relaxed and warm. My left foot is relaxed . . . and warm.

The warmth of my left foot spreads up into my left leg . . . My left leg is relaxed . . . and warm. My left leg is relaxed . . . and warm. My left leg is relaxed . . . and warm.

My feet and my legs are warm . . . My feet and legs are warm.

My hands and arms are warm . . . My hands and arms are warm.

My arms and legs are warm and relaxed . . . My arms and legs are connected by the steady rhythm of my breathing.

And I am relaxed . . . and warm. I am relaxed . . . and warm.

My forehead is cool . . . but my arms and my legs are warm. My hands and my feet are warm. Everything is connected together by the life-giving rhythm of my breathing.

I breathe deeply and completely.

I breathe deeply and completely.

I breathe deeply and completely.

The energy of my breathing circulates freely throughout my body. The relaxing warmth of my breathing flows throughout my body.

My fingertips are warm . . . My shoulders and back are warm . . . My toes are warm . . . My feet and my legs are warm.

I am . . . relaxed. I am . . . warm . . . and relaxed.

My mind is relaxed and comfortable . . . My whole body is quiet . . . but pulsing with life. I am at peace. I feel my body alive with its rhythms.

My mind is still . . . I am comfortable and still . . . I am calm and at peace . . . I am warm and relaxed . . . I am in perfect harmony.

Body, mind, and spirit . . . united by the steady rhythm of my breathing.

Pause

Continue with a visualization exercise or say the following:

As I continue to breathe deeply and comfortably, I prepare to return my awareness to my surroundings. I feel life and energy flowing through my body . . . yet I remain calm and relaxed.

Refreshed and renewed, I prepare to return to the challenges of my life . . . taking this warmth and peace with me.

Pause

Take as long as you need to return . . . then slowly stretch your arms and legs, your shoulders and neck. Allow your breathing to maintain its steady pace . . . as you begin to tune in to your surroundings.

When you are ready, open your eyes and notice what is around you . . . but take with you the warmth . . . and the peace . . . that you gave yourself during these moments.

Return to your day relaxed . . . renewed . . . refreshed . . . by the regular rhythm of your steady breathing.

Repeat the above instructions until everyone is alert.

Relaxation Training for Children

Author Unknown*

Time: 12 minutes

This entertaining relaxation script is perfect for children (and adults) because it teaches them how to tense and relax their muscles while utilizing their fantasy and imagination skills.

Start by introducing a few muscle groups at a time and add more as participants become familiar with this exercise and when they're able to remain still and keep their eyes closed for longer periods of time.

As always, feel free to modify this script in any way to make it more effective to your particular situation and audience. For example, you may have to repeat the instructions more often than what is written.

Script

Close your eyes . . . and relax.

Pretend you have a whole lemon in one of your hands. Squeeze it hard . . . Try to squeeze all the juice out. Feel how tight your hand and arm is as you squeeze.

Now drop the lemon . . . Feel the difference . . . Take another lemon and squeeze it. Feel the

35

tightness . . . Now drop the lemon and feel the relaxation.

Now pretend you have a whole lemon in your other hand . . . Squeeze it hard. Try to squeeze all the juice out. Feel how tight your hand and arm is as you squeeze.

Now drop the lemon . . . Feel the difference . . . Take another lemon and squeeze it. Feel the tightness . . . Now drop the lemon and feel the relaxation.

Pretend that you are a furry, lazy cat . . . which really wants to stretch. Stretch your arms in front of you . . . Raise them high above your shoulders. Feel the pull in your shoulders . . . Stretch higher.

Now let your arms drop by your sides . . . Feel the difference . . . Stretch again. Put your arms way out in front of you . . . Raise them over your head . . . Pull them way back . . . Now quickly drop them.

Keep your eyes closed . . . Remember, you are a lazy cat and are just stretching. You don't really want to wake up and see anything. Feel how good and warm and lazy it is to be relaxed.

Now pretend that you are a turtle . . . You are

sitting on a rock by a very peaceful pond, just relaxing in the warm sun.

Oh no! You sense danger. Pull your head into your house. Try to pull your shoulders up to your ears and push your head down into your shoulders . . . Hold in tight. It isn't easy to be a turtle in a shell.

The danger is past now. You can come out into the warm sunshine again. Once more, relax and feel the warm sun . . . Keep your eyes closed . . . Just take a few moments to relax . . .

Here it comes again! Pull your head back into your house and hold it tight. Protect yourself.

OK, you can come out again and relax . . . Notice how much better it feels to be relaxed than to be all tightened up.

Now pretend that you have a giant jawbreaker bubble gum in your mouth. It's very hard to chew. Bite down on it . . . Hard . . . Let your neck muscles help you . . . Now relax. Just let your jaw hang loose . . . Notice how good it feels to let your jaw drop.

OK, let's tackle that jawbreaker again . . . Bite down . . . Hard. Try to squeeze it out between your teeth. That's good. You're really tearing that gum up. Now relax again . . . Just let your jaw drop down. It feels good to let go and not have to fight that bubble gum.

OK, one more time. Really tear it up this time. Bite down . . . Hard as you can. Harder. Oh, you're really working hard . . . Good. Now relax . . . Try to relax your whole body . . . You've beaten the jawbreaker. Let yourself go as loose as you can.

Here comes a pesky fly. He has landed on your nose. Try to get him off without using your hands. Wrinkle up your nose. Make as many wrinkles in your nose as you can. Scrunch it up as hard as you can.

Good. You chased him away. Now you can relax your nose. Feel how good it is without the fly.

Oops, here he comes again. Right back to the middle of your nose. Shoo him away . . . Notice that when you scrunch up your nose, your cheeks and your mouth and your forehead and your eyes all help you and they get tight as well.

When you relax your nose, the rest of your face relaxes too and feels very good . . . Let your face go smooth, no wrinkles anywhere . . . Your face feels nice and smooth and relaxed.

Here comes a cute baby elephant . . . Oh no.

He's not watching where he's going. He doesn't see you sitting there in the grass and he's about to step on your stomach.

Don't move. You don't have time to get out of the way. Just get ready for him. Make your stomach very hard. Tighten up your stomach muscles. Hold it . . . It looks like he's going away. You can relax now. Let your stomach relax and be as soft as it can be . . . Feel how good that is.

Oh no, he's coming back. Tighten up again . . . Real hard. If he steps on you it won't hurt. Make your stomach like a rock . . . All right, he's moved away again. You can relax. Just get comfortable and feel relaxed in the warm sun in the open field.

This time, imagine that you want to squeeze through a narrow fence. You'll have to make yourself very skinny if you're going to make it through. Suck your stomach in. Try to squeeze it up against your backbone. Try to be as skinny as you can. You've got to get through.

Now relax . . . You don't have to be skinny now . . . Just relax and feel your stomach being warm and loose . . . OK, let's try to get through that fence now. Squeeze up your stomach. Make it touch your backbone. Get it real flat and tight. Get as skinny as you can. Hold tight now.

39

You've got to squeeze through . . .

Good. You got through that skinny little fence.
You can relax now . . . Settle back and let your
stomach come back out where it belongs.

You feel really good now. Let your stomach be
loose and relaxed, like a bowl of Jell-O . . .
You've done fine.

This time, pretend you are standing barefoot in
a big mud puddle. Squish your toes down deep
into the mud. Try to get your feet down to the
bottom of the mud puddle. You'll probably need
your legs to help you push. Push down, spread
your toes apart, and feel the mud squish up
between your toes. Keep squishing.

Now step out of the mud puddle. Relax your
feet. Let your toes go loose and feel how nice
that is . . . Just relax your toes and feet.

Step back into the mud puddle. Squish your toes
down. Let your leg muscles help. Try to squeeze
the puddle dry . . . OK. Come back out now.
Relax your toes . . . relax your feet . . . relax your
legs . . . It feels good to be relaxed, with no
tension anywhere. Just warm and tingly.

Pause

40

Continue with a visualization exercise or say the following:

Stay as relaxed as you can. Let your whole body go limp, and feel all your muscles relax . . . In a while, I will ask you to open your eyes and stretch.

As you go through the day, it is important to remember how good it feels to be relaxed.

Pause

Very slowly now, open your eyes and wiggle your arms and legs around. Stretch and get up slowly when you are ready.

Repeat the above instructions until everyone is alert.

* This script has been in Julie Lusk's files for over ten years, and she has been unable to locate the original author. If any reader knows the original author of the work, please advise the publisher so that the author can be acknowledged.

Nature and the Environment

This section contains a variety of guided meditations that will help deepen your ability to relax and sharpen your ability to visualize, whether you *visualize* by using your imagination to see, feel, smell, or hear the scenes described. When you practice using all your senses, your experience will be enriched.

Getting in touch with nature is soothing, inspiring, and healing. To get the most out of these visualizations, first take the time to thoroughly relax.

Remember to briefly describe the content of the guided visualization to the people you are working with. If a particular setting makes anyone uncomfortable, select a different script.

Finding Your Own Sacred Place

Michael Arloski

Time: 20 minutes

Participants are gently guided into a relaxed state of being and then given instructions for discovering and exploring a comfortable, personal sacred place.

Script

Allow yourself to relax while sitting in a comfortable chair that supports you, or by lying down on your back on a comfortable surface.

Close your eyes and become aware of your body . . . Scan your body from head to toe and visualize each part. See each part of your body in your minds eye.

Notice the feelings, or lack of feeling, that you experience as you do this . . . Don't work at it, let it happen . . . Give yourself permission to let go. Allow yourself to concentrate, but in a passive, very passive way.

This is a time to let go . . . a time to reconnect with yourself . . . and with the world of nature that you are a part of. This is a time to find that very special place where you can feel safe, calm, and quiet—where you can feel grounded with the earth.

Since time immemorial, peoples of all origins have valued and ritualized time alone in the wilderness as a key to understanding their personal journeys, and as a method for finding spiritual life paths.

Now, give yourself permission to access a deeper part of yourself, to relax and find your own sacred place.

Without changing it, become aware of your breath, the life-giving air of the universe that sustains us all. Follow a breath in through your nose, down into your lungs . . . and back out again.

Now take a deeper breath, drawing the air in through your nose and down in to fill your lungs completely, hold it . . . and then exhale. Imagine the tension flowing out with your breath.

Follow the motion of your own breathing . . . Let it set a rhythm for you; pace yourself with it.

Draw into yourself . . . the air, the breath of the world . . . Perhaps, you will want to say silently to yourself "I am" as you breathe in . . . and then "relaxed" as you breathe out.

"I am . . . relaxed"

Allow your next inhalation and exhalation to be just a little bit longer and deeper than the ones before.

With each successive breath, let your inhalation be just a bit longer, fuller and deeper than the last . . . Your exhalation just a bit slower, smoother, and more complete.

Do this until you are breathing in to your full capacity . . . and breathing out slowly and completely, until you have emptied your lungs of all their air.

Pause 10 seconds

Now let your breathing return to a natural and effortless rhythm, perhaps a bit deeper and fuller than usual.

Pause 10 seconds

Feel the earth's energy come in with each inhale . . . and the tension flow out and into the earth with each exhale. Allow the earth to absorb the tension for you.

Your thoughts now are turned inward and you feel at ease. Be aware of very few thoughts in your mind at all.

Pause

There are very special places on the planet
where the life force is more concentrated than at
other places. These are places of light, power,
healing, and creative energy, where location and
structure magnify spiritual intensity. These are
places of calm and tranquility.

In the quiet realm of your mind, allow yourself
to create an alliance with such a place. As you
slowly breathe the breath of the earth in and out,
begin to search for your place.

Create a landscape in your mind that fits with
the land where you live. If you live in flat land,
begin to picture that. If you live in a land of hills
or mountains, see them in your mind's eye. If
you live near water, start to picture that.

See or feel yourself quietly sitting or lying
down in a natural setting that is safe, calm, and
familiar. Allow yourself to flow into this quiet
space with each breath you take . . . Allow
yourself to float quietly into this scene as if you
were a white cloud floating in the blue sky
above. Picture yourself in harmony with the
place itself. Feel the support it has to give you.

Experience your land in the season it is right
now. Feel the warm sun heat your body, or a
cool breeze brush by your face . . . Smell the
fragrances of this place, the perfume of flowers,

the saltiness of the seashore, possibly the sweet smell of sage after a rain shower.

Whatever is present for your very own place . . . let it fill your nostrils and center you more fully on this land.

Explore this place with your other senses as well . . . Feel or see yourself reaching out with your sensitive fingertips and feeling the textures of this place. Feel the roughness, the smoothness. Touch and experience all the feelings and messages this place has for you.

Select something from this special place that you can allow yourself to taste; the water, a plant, perhaps a fruit. Something that delivers to you a pleasant taste . . . Smell and taste it now.

Let the flavor deepen your sense of being with this place.

Begin to look at this place from many different angles. If water is present, see this place from the level of the water itself, as though through the eyes of a frog.

This time, see it from the branches of any trees that might be there, like a squirrel would.

Now imagine soaring high above it all, seeing it

through the eyes of a hawk. Notice as you look and listen and use your other senses how this place is teeming with life.

Hear the sounds of humming insects, and singing birds . . . Hear the rush of the wind through the leaves and branches or blades of grass.

At every aspect of this scene there are other creatures engaged fully in the process of living . . . Feel the connection to those creatures that Native Americans call "all our relations."

Now simply settle into this sacred place. Feel its embrace . . . Breathe in its loving energy . . . and breathe out your love into it.

Pause for 1 minute

Slowly allow yourself to become aware of the space you are in.

Feel the earth that supports you, even if you are on a floor some distance from the surface of the earth. Acknowledge your connection to the earth that completely sustains you.

Allow yourself to remain grounded with the energy of the earth, energized by the breath of the life-giving air that surrounds us, and warmed by the sun that shines down on us all.

Go in peace with all our relations.

Pause

Become aware of your breath again, and breathe in deeply . . . Feel the energy flow in with that breath . . . You might wish to stretch as you breathe in.

Now quietly . . . gently . . . allow your eyelids to open.

Repeat the above instructions until everyone is alert.

Mountain Tops

Julie T. Lusk

Time: 8 minutes

A mountain top is the setting for this relaxing journey to relaxation and renewal.

Be sure to use some type of relaxation exercise before going on to this script.

Script

Imagine yourself on a mountain top. Allow yourself to be there right now . . . on top of a mountain . . . a beautiful, majestic mountain . . . a mountain that is blanketed with grass . . . wildflowers . . . and trees.

The air is cool and refreshing . . . gently blowing . . . alive and refreshing.

Looking down . . . see the grass that covers the ground. Each blade of grass is unique . . . a reflection of the uniqueness in all of us. A gentle breeze blows through the grass . . . the blades sway back and forth . . . easily and naturally.

Looking around, notice the delicate and beautiful wildflowers . . . a rainbow of colorful

flowers . . . yellow . . . red . . . purple, blue . . .
in a rainbow of colors . . . the wildflowers
poking their petals all around.

They are beautiful . . . inspirational.

Reflect now upon the relationship of the grass
and wildflowers . . . living and growing together
in their diversity . . . sharing the earth and all its
abundant resources . . . being nurtured and
cared for.

Notice the interplay of sunlight and shadows
upon the grass and flowers . . . constant, yet
everchanging . . . living and thriving together . . .
flourishing together . . . in unison.

Draw your attention to the trees . . . the majestic
and noble trees upon the mountain.

Notice their tree trunks . . . providing support
and strength. See the bark covering the trunk of
the tree . . . providing protection to the tree . . .
protecting its life force . . . fully and completely.

Reach out to touch the tree's protective
covering . . . What is it like?

Now notice the canopy of branches and leaves
towering up from the tree . . . reaching toward
the sky. Watch as the leaves and branches blow
gently in the breeze . . . Watch as the sunlight

shines down, creating patterns of light and shadow upon the leaves.

The leaves wave back and forth . . . dancing back and forth to the music of the breeze . . . creating the soothing sounds of the leaves blowing in the breeze . . . coming and going . . . cool and fresh . . . sweet.

The breeze blowing the leaves sounds soft . . . and then louder . . . the constant, yet ever-changing movement . . . the profound drama of nature.

Watch the leaves as they reach out toward the sky . . . the green leaves, the blue sky, the white clouds . . . the beautiful blue sky . . . rich and deep and blue . . . peaceful, calm. This scene is tranquil and blissful.

Now notice the view from up on this mountain top. Notice the earth . . . the mountains . . . the peaks and valleys . . . going on and on . . . on and on . . . above and beyond . . . stretching out toward the horizon.

Sitting upon this mountain . . . above it all . . . away from it all . . . calm and secure . . . at peace . . . you gain a new perspective of life on earth.

The grandeur of the mountains . . . their

breathtaking beauty . . . renewing and refreshing . . . are always there . . . always renewing . . . refreshing . . . fulfilling, the mountains.

Pause

Slowly now, bring your attention back to this place. Feel the floor beneath you . . . Take in a nice, deep breath and sigh it out . . . sigh all the way out. Stretch out whenever you are ready and open your eyes . . . feeling refreshed and renewed.

Repeat the above instructions until everyone is alert.

Caribbean Vacation

Patricia A. McPartland

Time: 10 minutes

This guided meditation promotes inner peace, beauty, renewal, and release of negativity. Participants are encouraged to feel connected and grounded to the universe.

Script

It is now time to stop talking and to settle down and be still. Let the inner voices of your mind become quiet.

As thoughts come in to your mind, simply let them float right on by. Briefly acknowledge their presence and let them pass.

Take in a deep breath . . . Now slowly exhale . . . Take in another deep and full breath . . . and exhale completely. Feel more and more peaceful and calm with each breath.

Let your breath return to a comfortable, relaxed, and normal rhythm.

Imagine that you are surrounded by white

light . . . The white light protects you and makes you feel safe and secure. Know that only good will come to you and only that which is good will come from you.

Visualize a beautiful ocean . . . Become aware of the colors of the water. You feel at one with the beauty and vastness of the ocean.

Listen to the sounds of the waves. Hear the waves as they come in, and as they go out . . . in . . . and out . . . in . . . and out. Listening to the sound of the waves, you feel completely at peace with yourself.

Now visualize a long, sandy beach . . . Walk along the beach and feel the sand against your feet . . . grounding you to the earth . . . connecting you to all others in the universe. You feel inner peace and strength.

As you walk along the beach feeling strong and connected, you find a deflated balloon. Imagine the balloon to be of any color you choose.

As you hold this balloon, you get in touch with the things that bother you . . . and fill your balloon with all your concerns as they occur to you. Fill your balloon with those issues that trouble you.

When your balloon is filled up with your

worries, let it go . . . release the balloon to the universe. Watch as the balloon, filled with your worries, floats up and away . . . Watch your balloon take off far into the sky, getting smaller and smaller as it floats up in the sky.

You feel certain that the universe will know how to take care of everything . . . You are now free of all those problems. You feel lighter, happier, full of joy and self-worth.

As you continue your walk on the beach you feel at one with all the beings in the universe and with everything and everyone in it . . . You are at peace with yourself and with others. You feel inner strength and inner joy knowing that you can always come back to this special place.

Pause

It is time to bring your experience to an end for now. Remember that you can re-create this experience anytime you wish to feel refreshed and free.

Bring your awareness back to your breath now. You feel alert and fresh with each breath you take in . . and release out. When you are ready, begin stretching, then open your eyes.

Repeat the above instructions until everyone is alert.

Mighty Pine

Irene O'Boyle

Time: 10 minutes

Participants take an imaginary walk into a grove of trees to find a mighty pine tree from which they draw strength and energy.

Be sure to use some type of relaxation exercise before going on to this script. Also, have participants hold a pinecone to enhance their experience.

Script

Relax and find a comfortable place . . . Close your eyes and let your responsibilities fade away for now . . . Let your imagination take you on a journey.

Your journey begins with a short refreshing walk into a grove of trees . . . As you enter the grove, you see a mighty pine towering above the others.

You stop a moment to marvel at its strength . . . You gaze in amazement at its large and stately branches blowing softly in the warm breeze.

As you get closer, you start to feel the cushion of

the fallen pine needles beneath your feet . . .
surrounding your feet in comfort . . . absorbing
all your pain. The many needles soften your
steps . . . lighten your body.

You feel drawn closer and closer to this
magnificent pine tree . . . Its strength pulls
you near . . . protects you.

As you sit at the base of the tree, you take a deep
cleansing breath . . . and another breath . . . and
another. The fresh air helps cleanse your fears,
your worries . . . and it gives you strength.

You feel strength slowly seeping into your
body . . . growing inside with every breath . . .
spreading throughout your body . . . seeping
into your head . . . into your neck . . . and
chest . . . down your arms . . . fingers . . . into
your abdomen . . . legs . . . feet . . . toes . . .
warming your entire body ever so powerfully.

The strong pine smell is invigorating . . .
energizing. The mighty pine is absorbing your
worries . . . fears . . . frustrations.

Pause

As the tree soaks up the warm breeze, you feel
yourself sway with the mighty branches . . .
Small birds have joined your journey and they
chatter freely.

The sights, sounds, and smells continue to give you strength . . . and you feel warm . . . and energized by the journey.

Slowly, you start to rise and head back to the place from which you started. As you leave, you again feel the cushion of the fallen pine needles under your feet . . . You smile as you think about coming to see this magnificent tree again.

Pause

When you are ready, open your eyes, stretch a glorious stretch, and feel energized and strong by the journey you have just taken.

Repeat the above instructions until everyone is alert.

Listening to Mother Earth

Julie T. Lusk

Time: 5 minutes

This script can help participants experience their connection to Mother Earth and learn from her wisdom.

Be sure to use some type of relaxation exercise before going on to this script. Expanding and Contracting *is recommended.*

Script

You find yourself lying outside on the ground. Notice your surroundings.

Are you in a grassy, sandy, or rocky area . . . Notice the time of day . . . Become aware of all the colors . . . the different shades of blue . . . green . . . red . . . orange . . . and yellow. Now notice all the sounds. Do you hear wind . . . or water?

Feel now your earth mother beneath you, supporting you . . . She is very old, wise, and alive. She has always been there for you and will always be there for you.

Feel her holding you . . . comforting you.

Allow yourself to melt into her, feeling her power and energy, certain that she is alive and sharing her life force with you.

Give yourself over to her completely. Feel your spirit become one with her, and feel her spirit become one with you . . . A sense of tranquility and harmony comes to you.

Breathe in her life-giving force, becoming even more in tune with her . . . Feel Mother Earth share her vibrations and wisdom with you . . . Absorb her energy. Feel it surround and pour through you.

You begin to realize that she has something she would like to share with you . . . Open up your mind and heart and listen for her personal message to you.

Pause for 1 to 2 minutes

Once again, become aware of the ground beneath you. Notice your head, back, arms, and legs against the floor. Begin stretching, and whenever you are ready, open your eyes.

Repeat the above instructions until everyone is alert.

Flying

John Heil

Time: 20 minutes

This script begins with a relaxation exercise that emphasizes the feelings of heaviness and lightness to help participants more fully experience the imagery of flying.

Be creative in making variations to the script. For example, have participants imagine slowly descending a great height, twisting and twirling as if they were feathers; or riding updrafts as soaring birds, subtly changing their movements to get the best ride.

Script

Wiggle around until you find a way of sitting or lying down that is completely comfortable. Then close your eyes and think about your hands. Feel the weight of them . . . Feel the bones inside them . . . Feel the muscles that move the bones.

Now make a fist with your hands and clench tightly. Hold your hands tightly . . . hold . . . hold . . . hold. Now relax and feel the soothing, tingling sensation of relaxation come into your hands.

Now draw up your arms and tighten both your

biceps as tight as you can. Hold them tightly . . .
hold . . . hold . . . hold. Now relax and feel the
tension drain out of your arms.

Now shrug your shoulders . . . pushing them up
as if you were pushing them through your ears.
Hold them tightly there . . . hold . . . hold . . .
hold. Now let them go and feel all the tension
drain out of your body.

Continuing to keep your eyes closed, open your
mouth as far as it will go, stretching the muscles
at the corners of your mouth as far as they will
go. Hold your mouth open . . . hold . . . hold . . .
hold. Relax and enjoy the tingling feeling as the
tension in your mouth dissolves.

Now press your tongue against the roof of your
mouth and tighten your jaw muscles. Press
tightly and hold . . . hold . . . hold . . . hold. Now
relax, feeling the tension flow out of your face.

Now tighten the muscles of your chest, stomach,
and abdomen. Hold them tense . . . hold . . .
hold . . . hold. Now let them go, feeling the
soothing sensation of relaxation pour in.

Now tense the muscles of your thighs by
straightening your legs. Hold them tightly . . .
hold . . . hold . . . hold. Now relax your thighs.
Let all of the tension drain out of them.

Now add to your general state of relaxation by performing a *body check* . . . You may do this by sending a message to relax to any part of your body in which you become aware of tension or discomfort. In this way, you can finely tune your body to an enhanced state of relaxation by meeting patterns of tension and discomfort as they arise.

Begin by focusing your attention on your feet. If they are tense, send a message to them to let go. If they are relaxed, encourage them to relax even further.

Now do the same for your hands. Again encourage them to be free of tension by sending a message of relaxation.

Repeat this process for your face . . . and head . . . taking great care to free the many muscles there from tension.

Now focus your attention on your whole body . . . Let your mind be relaxed, but alert, continuously monitoring your entire muscular system. And now be prepared to dissolve patterns of tension and discomfort as they arise.

Pause for 30 seconds

Now allow your mind's eye to open. Notice that you are standing before a staircase situated in the middle of a large, dimly lit room. As you move to the first step, you notice a subtle feeling of heaviness beginning to come over you. And on the second step, this feeling of heaviness increases.

Moving now to the third step, you feel heavier still. And as you move on to the fourth and fifth steps, this feeling of heaviness becomes stronger and continues to increase as you move on to the sixth . . . seventh . . . and eighth steps.

And on the ninth and tenth steps, your body feels extremely heavy.

You have now come to a sparsely furnished room. The floor in the room is covered with a deep pile carpet . . . You begin to move slowly toward a couch located just a short distance away in the middle of the room.

As you take your first step, your feet begin to sink deeply into the carpet . . . And with the second step, your feet sink more deeply . . . The strands of the carpet brush against your ankle. And taking your third and fourth steps . . . you continue to sink more and more deeply.

With each succeeding step, you sink more deeply into the carpet, till finally you arrive at the foot of the couch.

Your body feels incredibly heavy, but you turn

your body around and allow yourself to fall softly and slowly onto the couch.

This couch is perfect for you. As you sink more and more deeply into the couch, you begin to feel it support your body . . . But you are so heavy that you continue to sink deeper and deeper, down and down . . . till finally you come to rest with your head and neck and your entire body perfectly supported.

As you lie there, your body becomes still heavier, sinking more and more deeply into the couch.

And now, the dim light in the room begins to flicker . . . the colors become muted . . . the details of the surroundings grow hazy and indistinct.

And as the image of the room around you continues to disappear, that feeling of heaviness begins to dissolve . . . slowly at first . . . and now more and more rapidly . . . till you find yourself becoming lighter . . . and lighter . . . and lighter still . . . feeling weightless . . . till finally . . . a feeling of floating comes over you . . . as you continue all the while to grow lighter . . . and lighter still.

And as the haze that has obscured the vision of your mind's eye begins to dissipate . . . you find

that you are floating high in·the sky . . . far
above the ground below, far from the humdrum
of everyday life.

On you float . . . freely and easily . . . through
the calm, still world of the sky, which is now
dotted with bright white fluffy clouds.

And growing accustomed to this lighter than air
feeling, you find that with an imaginary roll of
your head or twist of your shoulders, you may
direct your movement through space . . . able to
move up or down, left or right, at will.

And now you drop your head and shoulders
and move into an exhilarating descent . . . until
you gradually level off by pulling your head
back and up.

Lifting your head and shoulders, you begin to
ascend slowly . . . till with growing confidence
you arch your back and move into a steep,
climbing ascent . . . and then once again level off.

And then you begin to descend again and with
a roll of your head, you bank to the left and soar
into a cloud.

Sheltered for a time in the dark interior of
the cloud, you experience a cool, soothing
sensation . . . which at once invigorates and
refreshes you . . . as you drift on and on. And

then in an instant, you are out of the cloud and once again in the warm sunlight.

Arching your back, and rolling your shoulders to the right, you begin a gradual banking ascent . . . with the warm, penetrating sun shining on your back . . . removing the slightest hint of chill left from your journey through the cloud.

Breathing easily and deeply, take some time to experience the freedom of flight . . . and on you soar . . . passive . . . relaxed . . . and at ease.

Pause for 1 to 2 minutes.

When you are ready, count silently to yourself from five to one. When you reach the count of one . . . you may open your eyes and begin to stretch, feeling relaxed . . . exhilarated . . . and refreshed.

Repeat the above instructions until everyone is alert.

Hot Tubbing

Julie T. Lusk

Time: 5 minutes

Participants experience feelings of peace and understanding by imagining they are lounging in an outdoor hot tub.

Be sure to use some type of relaxation exercise before going on to this script.

Script

Imagine yourself stepping into an outdoor hot tub . . . The temperature of the tub is perfect. You feel very safe as you sit in it . . . comforted by the toasty warm water that surrounds you.

Feel yourself letting go of tension, and your body relaxing . . . You feel comfortable and warm, through and through . . . more and more.

All sense of tiredness melts away . . . your mind settles down . . . and you feel peaceful and calm . . . serene.

As you relax even more, feel a gentle breeze blowing gently across your skin. When you listen closely, you can hear the tinkling sound of wind chimes . . . melodic . . . musical.

Looking around, you notice the setting sun . . . The sky glows beautifully . . . Billowy clouds float smoothly overhead. Watch them turn golden . . . copper . . . purple . . . and red.

The sky is turning darker and darker, the moon begins to shine, and stars light up the night.

As you gaze overhead at the moon and stars, you feel a solid sense of your connection to the universe . . . Sitting there secure and at peace, reflect on this feeling that everything is as it should be . . . and in perfect order.

Pause

Draw your attention back to this room. Picturing where you are . . . begin to stretch and become alert. When you are ready, open your eyes and sit up.

Repeat the above instructions until everyone is alert.

Inner Answers

Using the guided imagery exercises in this section will help you listen to what you already know. In other words, you will awaken your intuition to help you be consistent and in alignment with your own inner, individual truth.

These scripts are written to unlock your creative potential, provide you with insights, help you see patterns and possibilities, and understand yourself better. In order for this to happen, it is crucial to relax your body and quiet your mind first. So be sure to use a relaxation exercise whenever you are instructed to do so.

Read *Awakening Intuition* by Frances E. Vaughan for more information about accessing your intuitive self.

boundaries, protection, positive body image, healing, and unconditional love. (15 minutes)

Body, Mind, Soul   p. 86
Help your clients get in touch with their body, mind, and soul while they increase personal awareness and create personal strength and well-being. (8 minutes)

Visiting Your Heart's House   p. 90
In this script, participants equip themselves to meet life's challenges by receiving insightful and helpful gifts from an ancient chest located in their heart's house. (18 minutes)

Cruise Meditation

Julie T. Lusk

Time: 8 minutes

This script helps participants receive special messages from their own personal inner guide.

Be sure to use some type of relaxation exercise before going on to this script.

Script

Close your outer eyes and open your inner ones. As you relax more and more, find yourself aboard a boat during your favorite time of the day . . . Notice the boat's size . . . shape . . . and color.

As you float along in your boat, you see the gorgeous, sparkling color of the water as it reflects the sunlight.

In the distance, you see an island, and you find yourself being drawn towards it . . . As you get closer and closer to the island, you see that it is covered with colorful flowers. Your boat comes to rest on the shore and you step out onto the island.

Notice the brilliant and diverse colors, shapes, and sizes of the flowers . . . You breathe in their luscious fragrance and admire their beauty.

As you wander through this garden paradise, you see a path and feel an irresistible urge to follow it . . . You decide to walk down the path.

As you walk along, you are fully aware of the brilliant colors . . . the clear and crisp air . . . and the solitude of your environment.

You come to a clearing, which you soon realize is an entrance to a quiet shrine.

You enter the shrine and immediately feel an overwhelming sense of peace and calm . . . You feel as if you belong. It's heavenly.

You sit down and someone who is a personal and wise guide for you appears at the outer edge of the clearing . . . possibly someone you know now, maybe someone you used to know, or perhaps a new friend.

You feel as if you know this person very well . . . You feel perfectly comfortable and in harmony with your surroundings and with this long-lost friend.

Your friend asks if you would be open to receiving an important message, perhaps an answer to a question you may have, perhaps some wise advice that will benefit you. If you agree, you nod your head.

As you listen to your message, you feel a sense of unity between the message, your friend, and yourself.

Pause

Now it is time to say good-bye to this special guide in whatever way you choose.

Gathering yourself together, you stand up and walk back along the path toward the boat. You feel happy, harmonious, and blessed.

Now draw your attention back to this room. On the count of five you will open your eyes and stretch, feeling energized, refreshed, and happy. 1 . . . 2 . . . 3 . . . 4 . . . 5. Open your eyes and stretch.

Repeat the above instructions until everyone is alert.

Imagery for Nurturing Your Inner Child

Elaine M. Sullivan

Time: 10 minutes

In this guided imagery, each participant is invited to meet and lovingly nurture his or her inner child.

Script

Begin by focusing on your breathing . . . be aware of your own rhythm . . . As you exhale, imagine letting go of the stress in your body.

Be aware of your breathing . . . and with your mind's eye, scan your body for areas where you hold stress.

Feel these areas relax and let go. Feel your entire body relax . . . and let go. Allow your mind to let go of your thoughts, worries, and concerns.

You are completely relaxed . . . in mind . . . and in body. Imagine a soft breeze blowing over your body . . . helping you to let go even further . . . Feel the gentle caressing breeze. Imagine yourself deeply at peace.

See yourself leaving this room and going to a place in nature where you love to be . . . Feel yourself in this beautiful place. Gaze at your surroundings.

Smell the odors, the fragrances of this place . . . Touch your surroundings. Feel the feelings deep inside . . . as you find yourself becoming more and more peaceful, being alone with nature.

Find a space where you can lie down. Close your eyes and be aware of yourself alone in this place . . . You are alone and at peace. In the stillness you hear the beating of your heart. Gaze at the beauty around you.

In the distance you see a child coming toward you. You watch the child approach, noticing something very familiar about the child. As the child draws near, you become aware that this child is you . . . the child who lives inside of you.

Gazing upon the face of this little girl . . . this little boy . . . you see clearly what this child needs . . . what this child longs for. You are aware of this child's physical needs . . . emotional needs . . . intellectual . . . spiritual . . . and social needs.

You see the child so clearly . . . realizing so deeply what this little boy or little girl needs. As the child reaches out to you . . . you gather him

or her in your arms. You nurture the child in
ways he or she has always longed to be nurtured.

You say to the child what he or she has longed to
hear. You forgive . . . You give permission . . .
You listen to whatever the child has to say to you.

Take a few minutes to nurture your inner child.

Pause for 1 to 2 minutes

Look deeply into the eyes of this child and make
one promise to the child that you will keep.

Allow the child to merge with you . . . for this
little boy, this little girl lives within you every day
and every night. You are the nurturer . . . You are
the nurturer who invites this child to feel loved
and cared for.

Pause

Now be still and pay attention to your
breathing . . . When you are ready, gently bring
yourself back to the room. Stretch . . . move your
legs and arms . . . yawn . . . and open your eyes.

Repeat the above instructions until everyone is alert.

Your Private Space

Judy Fulop

Time: 15 minutes

This visualization works well with individuals in weight classes and in other classes dealing with the need for boundaries, protection, positive body image, healing, and unconditional love.

Be sure to use some type of relaxation exercise before going on to this script.

Script

Picture yourself in the woods. All around you the air smells fresh and cool.

Feel the warmth of the sunshine . . . Feel the gentle breeze as it blows across your face . . . Hear the birds singing and the sounds of leaves rustling in the wind.

As you look around and take in the sights, find a path that leads through the forest between the trees and wildflowers . . . If there is no path, make a path of your own and start walking down it.

As you stroll along, smell the cool and clean air,

hear the wind blowing gently past your ear, and feel the cool breeze against your body.

Now look down the path and notice that it leads through the forest to a less dense area . . . In the distance, you begin to see the outline of a small village.

As you get closer to the village, the path becomes wider and turns into a road . . . Look at the houses standing to each side of the road. The houses have street numbers and names on them, and they look familiar.

Head down the road until you find the house with your name on it . . . When you find your house, stand outside and look at its exterior, knowing that this is your dream house, the house you always wanted.

When you are ready, go up to the door . . . take out your key, and insert it into the lock. As you open the door, look inside your house. What colors do you see? What do you smell? What do you sense? . . . Are the floors wood or are they covered with rugs and carpet? Is the lighting bright or subdued?

Walk through your house, noting the furnish-ings, the smells, and the sights in this home of your creation.

Pause by each room until you find your favorite room . . . This is your special room, and it is decorated exactly the way you want.

Go into your room . . . Note the colors . . . the furniture . . . and the light in this room . . . this room that belongs to you.

Now find the area of the room that looks most comfortable. Take some time to sit or lie down in this area and relax for awhile . . . Imagine that you have a pillow, blanket, or some special object to help you relax.

Now take a deep breath and let your body sink into this special place . . . Allow your shoulders, head, chest, hips, thighs, feet, and other parts of your body to slow down and relax.

Pause 20 seconds

From this relaxed position, picture yourself walking toward a full-length mirror . . . Slowly look into this mirror . . . As you peer into the mirror, allow yourself to look at this person in the mirror as you would your best friend.

Begin looking at your feet and knees. Lovingly look at and send energy to these areas.

Move your eyes to your thighs and hips, again sending love and acceptance to the body of this very special friend, your friend.

Move on to your waist, stomach, and chest,
smiling at your reflection . . . unconditionally
sending love to your body.

Continue up to your neck and your face, gently
smiling at the person you see in the mirror.

Thank the person for being there for you . . .
Thank this person for being exactly who they
are . . . and begin to allow yourself to see past
the physical body into the energy of their
mind . . . and their spirit. Thank this image for
being more than a body.

Continue to look at the image in the mirror.

Pause 10 seconds

Think about something that you have always
longed to hear and need to hear said to you.

Looking at your image, express that message in
any manner you wish, perhaps with a smile,
words, or a general feeling of unconditional
acceptance and love.

Pause 15 seconds

Allow yourself to say . . . I love you, even if . . .

Pause 15 seconds

While you are still looking into the mirror, take

your arms and wrap them around yourself, and give yourself a hug . . . Hold this hug for as long as you can, and soak up all the good feelings from it that you can.

Feel yourself being loved and cared for just as you are . . . Hold this moment and know that this moment is yours to keep and cherish forever.

When you are ready, permit yourself to look into this mirror one more time . . . Is there anything else you would like to say or hear? Spend a few more moments saying what you most need to hear.

Pause 20 seconds

Allow yourself to come back to your comfortable place in your favorite room . . . Give yourself some time in this place to take in what you have experienced.

Pause 10 to 15 seconds

Know that you can come to this room whenever you like and no one will enter this room and be with you unless you invite them . . . This is your own private space and only you know where to find this room.

Knowing that you can come back, imagine yourself getting up slowly and looking around

this room . . . Walk out and close the door
behind you, knowing that you can come back to
this house and your special room at any time.

Find the door that leads out of the house, lock it
and begin to walk down the road . . . past the
other houses until you reach the path that leads
through the forest.

As you continue to walk on the path, allow
yourself to feel the breeze . . . see the rich
colors . . . and hear the different sounds of
the birds and other life in the forest.

Pause

Allow yourself to carry with you the love and
acceptance you felt in your special room of your
private place.

As you continue on the path, find the place
where you entered the forest and slowly come
back to this room. Stretch whenever you are
ready, and open your eyes.

Repeat the above instructions until everyone is alert.

Body, Mind, Soul

Julie T. Lusk

Time: 8 minutes

Help your clients get in touch with their body, mind, and soul while they increase personal awareness and create personal strength and well-being.

Begin with some type of relaxation exercise before going on to this script.

Script

Breathe deeply, fully, rhythmically, slowly, and completely . . . Cleanse and refresh all your internal organs and glands.

Feel the fresh air bringing oxygen to your blood and your brain . . . And breathe out all the accumulated wastes and tensions.

Focus your attention on my voice . . . Allow yourself to be relaxed, receptive, yet very alert. You are becoming perfectly relaxed, calm, peaceful, and tranquil.

You are warm and tingly as you feel yourself sinking into the surface that supports you. Expect and accept harmony and peace.

It is time to let go of all tension: physical . . . mental . . . emotional . . . and spiritual. To give your mind, body, and spirit a rest.

As thoughts come to mind, briefly acknowledge them and let them slip on by. In any way that you wish, release all negative thoughts and feelings.

Your body feels strong, vital, and whole . . . full of health. Feel, experience, and express your healthy body.

Your thoughts are free, easy, and clear. Feel, experience, and express your healthy mind.

You feel perfectly balanced. Feel, experience, and express your healthy spirit.

Feel yourself absorb and radiate physically, mentally, emotionally, and spiritually with wholeness . . . Your body, mind, and spirit are in perfect harmony, perfect balance.

Feel surrounded, enfolded, protected . . . soothed . . . refreshed . . . calm, blissful, whole, and joyful. Harmony, peace, and tranquility come to you . . . Your mind, body, and spirit are perfectly integrated and balanced. You are in tune with the universe.

As you relax more and more, focus your awareness on your inner self, your innermost core. Recognize, experience, and honor your internal source of well-being.

In any way that you wish, nourish your inner self and fill your body temple with love and balance.

Feel a light radiating from deep within your body . . . Absorb it completely . . . Savor, nourish, acknowledge, and express love for this permanent, everlasting spiritual power source.

Feel your inner spiritual center begin to glow . . . Experience it spreading all over your body . . . from the tip of your head to the soles of your feet . . . and now spreading throughout your entire being, physically, emotionally, mentally and spiritually.

Turn your attention to your family and friends.

Bless and love them one by one as you imagine them being surrounded, protected, and healed by the healing light.

Pause 1 to 2 minutes

Gently shift your attention back to your own body and soul, your being. Draw your attention back to this room, stretch, and open your eyes.

Repeat the above instructions until everyone is alert.

Visiting Your Heart's House

Tom Ferguson

Time: 18 minutes

In this script, participants equip themselves to meet life's challenges by receiving insightful and helpful gifts from an ancient chest located in their heart's house.

The length and meaning of this visualization exercise can be varied by choosing to open one, several, or all of the special presents.

Script

Begin by letting yourself become quiet. Close your eyes . . . allow yourself to settle down . . . and sit in silence for a moment.

Now bring your attention to your breath. As you breathe out, imagine that any stress in your body is passing out with the exhaled air.

Feel the stress passing out of your body and drifting far . . . far away . . . leaving you refreshed . . . happy . . . and very relaxed.

Let yourself be as comfortable as you're willing to allow yourself to be . . . There's no place you need to go right now. Nothing that you need to do. No problems that you need to solve.

Just let yourself relax. Let yourself relax even more . . . as your eyelids grow heavier and heavier . . . and your breathing becomes deeper . . . slower . . . and more regular.

Allow all the immediate worries and preoccupations of the day to slip away.

Imagine that you are now walking along a path in the country. You can feel the dirt under your feet . . . You can hear the birds in the trees on either side of the path . . . The sun is shining. A mild, pleasant breeze is blowing . . . and you feel very happy and content to be here. This is a very special time for you . . . for you are going to visit your heart's house.

At last you see it through the trees ahead, a house that exactly expresses your own tastes and preferences . . . A house that is perfectly suited to you. Every door and window . . . every piece of furniture . . . every color is exactly as you would have chosen.

Take a good look around and explore your heart's house.

Pause 20 to 30 seconds

You return now to your favorite room, where you find a large, ancient chest . . . You kneel down and open the chest. You discover, to your wonder and surprise, that the whole huge container is crammed full of presents . . . presents just for you.

They are presents from the most wise . . . centered . . . empowered part of yourself.

And so you begin to open the packages . . . And you discover that each one is a gift designed to help you accomplish the most important tasks and goals belonging to this period of your life.

The first present is something you can wear. Perhaps it is a medal or special insignia . . . or a hat or T-shirt with a message or picture on it . . . or maybe it's a special pair of footwear for getting to where you want to go.

If you wish, open this present now.

Pause 10 to 15 seconds

The next present is a book . . . Perhaps it is a real book that contains key information that you need to know . . . or an important book you've read in the past . . . or a vision for a book that will be given to *you* to write . . . or a symbolic book, with a special meaning only you will understand.

If you wish, take some time to look through this special book.

Pause 10 to 15 seconds

The next present is a tool or a piece of equipment, a profound and powerful piece of technology . . . old or new. It is something that will allow you to accomplish the things you are destined to accomplish during this period of your life . . . It could be a tool, a computer, a piece of athletic equipment, a paintbrush, maybe a musical instrument.

You may examine this tool if you wish.

Pause 10 to 15 seconds

The next present is a frame containing the pictures or photographs of one or more people . . . These are people who have been, or will be, helpful to you during this period of your life. They may be real, contemporary people . . . or they may be imaginary or spiritual beings . . . or great teachers . . . or people from other times . . . or figures from your past . . . or people you have yet to meet.

If you wish, spend a few moments looking at the photographs.

Pause 10 to 15 seconds

The next present is a neon sign in all your favorite colors. It spells out a phrase, sentence, or slogan that has a special meaning for you . . .

It bears a message that will be important for you to remember during this period in your life.

If you wish, you can tuck this sign away in your mind's eye, where you will be able to retrieve it and switch it on, whenever it is needed.

Pause 10 to 15 seconds

The next present is a telephone . . . This is a special telephone you can use to talk to anyone you wish to talk to at any time. You can use it to talk to real people. You can use it to talk to your inner advisor . . . You can use it to talk to any great spiritual figure who has special meaning for you. You can even use it to talk to your wounded inner child . . . or other repressed or hidden parts of yourself with which you might normally find it difficult to communicate.

You can use this special telephone now to call anyone you wish.

Pause 10 to 15 seconds

The next present is a symbol of your link to the natural world . . . It may be a living or spirit animal, or a pet. It may be a guardian animal who serves as your advisor . . . It may be a plant, a tree, a garden, a rock, a body of water, or a very special place . . . It may be some other creature or object that represents your special connection to the natural world.

Open this present if you wish.

Pause 10 to 15 seconds

The next present is a slide viewer, complete with a slide that is a vision of your future. A vision of you and your key friends, family members, and colleagues in a future situation in which you are doing what you most want and need to do.

If you like, you may view this slide now.

Pause 10 to 15 seconds

The next present is another photograph, a photo of yourself as a child . . . The child in this photo appears particularly vital . . . relaxed . . . and alive . . . for this is your playful . . . magical inner child, who is capable of great affection . . . intense curiosity . . . and is overflowing with the joy of life.

This photo is a symbol and link to all the forgotten or undiscovered possibilities that lie within.

Pause for 5 to 10 seconds

And then . . . at the bottom of the chest, you find the final present. This present, given to you by your own heart, is an object of great value, because it is a token of the power that lies within

you. The power to successfully deal with the
tasks and goals and challenges that belong to
this present period of your life.

As you look down at this final gift, you realize
that you are now feeling a calm assurance that
you will be able to walk this section of your own
personal path with a new vigor and a new
confidence . . . You know that the power and the
knowledge and everything else you will need to
know lies firmly and eternally within you, and is
available to you at any time.

Take some time to examine this final gift.

Pause 30 seconds

These gifts that you've discovered are truly gifts
from yourself . . . You have created them just as
they have appeared to you. They all lie
within . . . and are a part of you. You can return
to them, use them, and find other important
gifts at any time.

Pause

Now gradually return your attention to your
breathing.

Feel the air passing out and passing in. Feel
your fingers . . . and your toes as you gradually,
slowly begin to wiggle and stretch them.

Stretch your shoulders and arms . . . Open your mouth and stretch your jaw muscles . . . stretch your neck, from side to side.

And when you are ready, gradually, slowly open your eyes.

Repeat the above instructions until everyone is alert.

SECTION FOUR Healing

The mind and body are one, and what you believe and feel are reflected in your body. Sometimes your thoughts may lead to illness, aches, and pains; and other times, they can lead to exhilarating feelings of joy, pleasure, and peacefulness. Likewise, the condition of your body and the way it is feeling affect your thoughts. This is why it is impossible to worry when you feel relaxed.

Much of the benefits derived from the following healing imageries come from the necessary first step of calming and centering the body and mind. Therefore, it is important to perform a relaxation exercise whenever a script calls for one.

Read the works of Bernie Siegel, Jeanne Achterberg, Joan Borysenko, Patrick Fanning, and Deepak Chopra for an in-depth look at how and why healing imageries work.

Healing Firemen   **p. 100**
This visualization was developed for aiding in the healing process for any illness. It is particularly well-suited for cancer patients who are receiving radiation treatment or taking drugs. (12 minutes)

At Peace with Pain   **p. 105**
This visualization is designed to help meet the challenge of severe and persistent pain. It relies on the paradox of

acceptance and surrender as a way of gaining power, not of giving up. (20 minutes)

Pond of Love P. 112

In this script, participants sit beside an imaginary pond that radiates love. Endless variations can be created by substituting different characteristics and virtues radiating from the pond. For instance, the pond may be full of peace, understanding, or forgiveness. You may also want to let participants choose the characteristics on their own. (8 minutes)

Inner Smile p. 115

This gentle relaxation exercise has its roots in Zen meditation and will leave participants feeling inner harmony and happiness. (10 minutes)

Thoughts Library p. 120

This script can help participants control wandering, stressful, distracting thoughts by having them exchange these thoughts for relaxing ones. Participants visualize putting away unwanted thoughts in a book with vinyl see-through pages and then opening up another imaginary book to experience a relaxing and beautiful ocean scene. (15 minutes)

Healing Firemen

Bob Fellows

Time: 12 minutes

This visualization was developed for aiding in the healing process for any illness. It is particularly well-suited for cancer patients who are receiving radiation treatment or taking drugs.

Because of the nature of such treatments, people undergoing them often view them as a negative force in their bodies. A person who sees treatment this way and resists it is only adding stress to an already stressful situation. This script can help such people mentally and emotionally accept the treatment, which will help relieve the stress and possibly enhance the effectiveness of the treatment because the patient will be seeing it as a positive force.

If you are using this script for people undergoing radiation treatment, you can teach them to perform the relaxation part while they are sitting in the waiting room. And later, when the radiation machine is moving over them, they can visualize the firemen spraying the white fluid in their bodies. Tell them to imagine the firemen moving in the same direction and at the same speed as the machine, even if it moves back and forth several times.

The image of the white fluid represents white blood cells, which are responsible for removing cancerous cells from the body. It is better for participants to focus on the healing aspects of the fluid rather than on the firemen and the impurities the fluid is washing out.

Participants can finish the healing portion of the exercise when they are back in the waiting room or at their homes.

Script

If you can, lie down with your arms and legs straight so that energies can flow freely up and down your body. Use whatever method you prefer for calming your body, whether it is a form of progressive relaxation, a series of deep breaths to slow down your heartbeat and center yourself, or some visual image.

If you are using this script with a group, perform some type of relaxation exercise, then proceed with the visualization.

Now see your body as a hollow shell, an open and hollow shell . . . let it be empty and hollow for now . . . Make your body hollow for a while so that you can form a clear picture of the cleansing and healing process.

From nowhere, three to six firemen appear, all dressed in white and carrying white fire hoses. Let them be men or women, or both. It isn't important to spend time looking at their faces and wondering who they are. After all, they are very small.

Let your awareness go to your head. Watch . . . feel . . . and/or hear the firemen carefully spraying a white liquid all over the inside of your body, starting at your head and moving downward.

As they progress down your body, they can split up to enter your arms at the same time that some of them enter your torso.

Just imagine that they are hosing down the whole inside of your body equally and thoroughly, washing it completely clean.

Feel the soles of your feet open to the atmosphere.

The white liquid and impurities that may be picked up move downward until they leave your body through the soles of your feet . . . Or, if you like, you can visualize them disappearing into thin air.

Feel that this white liquid is cleansing all impurities out of your body . . . Just imagine that the thorough cleansing leaves your body fresh and sparkling.

When the firemen are finished doing their work, they will simply disappear as magically as they appeared . . . Let them go when you are ready, and then visualize your body in its normal state once again.

All the impurities have left through the soles of your feet . . . Your internal organs were there the whole time, and of course they were also cleansed. You just made your body hollow for a while so that you could form a clear picture of the firemen and the white liquid. The firemen were actually moving right through all the parts of the body as if they were spirits.

See and feel that your body is back to normal and completely cleansed . . . Bring your awareness back to your head, and see the top of your head open to the atmosphere.

Focus on your breathing and feel that with each breath, you bring positive, healing energy into your body through the top of your head.

Feel this energy come down into your head . . . filling your head and face with energy.

Continue bringing your awareness down your body, feeling the energy move further and further . . . filling your body with life-giving energy, all the way down to the tips of your toes.

Pause

Reflect for a moment on the integrity and healing powers of your body.

The natural healing forces which come into play at the time of illness are stronger than the illness. The body's integrity and intelligence is constantly guiding it to a normal, healthy condition, and the illness will eventually fail in its weak attempts to disorganize the body.

103

Each breath, each moment is bringing you closer to the healing process that is your life.

Pause

It is time to come back to the here and now. When you are ready, open your eyes and stretch.

Repeat the above instructions until everyone is alert.

At Peace with Pain

John Heil

Time: 20 minutes

This visualization is designed to help meet the challenge of severe and persistent pain. It relies on the paradox of acceptance and surrender as a way of gaining power, not of giving up.

Being at peace with severe pain is difficult by nature. Fortunately, pain can often be pushed from awareness by using relaxation and imagery exercises found in this book. If other exercises don't help, however, try using this script. Participants should try out this exercise several times before deciding if it helps or not. Sometimes the appeal of the images grows with repeated experience. Selected words or images that are not congruent with the individual's personal imagery may be eliminated, with or without the substitution of other imagery.

Script

And now you begin your journey inward to the place where there is peace with pain.

You are in the midst of the swirling, screeching wind and water of the storm of pain . . . a giant hurricane that blows all around you.

And you will pass through the storm to a place that is like the eye of a hurricane . . . where there is comfort and calm within the storm. You will travel across unfamiliar and challenging terrain to a special place.

You will move toward this place without map or compass, at times keenly aware of your surroundings . . . at other times, just fixed on your goal . . . that special place within . . . where there is peace with pain.

You are driven by the power within you, which is greater than the fury of the storm of pain that swirls all around . . . seeking that special place within.

You begin your journey and travel on and on . . . on and on . . . on and on . . . until, finally, you arrive at the threshold of this place within.

A wooden door stands before you . . . It has a deep, rich grain and appears to be completely smooth . . . You want to step through this door, but you notice no doorknob or handle.

You fix your eyes on the door and look deeply into the grain of the wood. At first you feel bewildered . . . but then you sense the door will open for you when you are ready.

You wait . . . You fix your eyes once again on the door . . . and focus on the grain of the wood. Feeling a sense of calm . . . of inner strength . . .

you sense that the door will open . . . and, in an instant, it does.

You are transported past a swirling, screeching, tearing, electric, burning, pounding wall . . . to a place of peace and quiet . . . where it is calm and quiet, away from the swirling and screaming . . . away from the tearing and throbbing.

You remain aware of the storm . . . but it seems far away. Deep within you, you know that the harder the storm pounds and crashes . . . the harder it tears and flashes . . . the more secure you become in this special place.

Your breathing is calm and relaxed . . . slow, deep, and regular. You are feeling calm and quiet.

Now, aware of your surroundings, you notice that this place is strangely familiar . . . At once it is both like a place where you have been before and a place that is new to you . . . a place where you feel peace and security . . . and where there are opportunities for discovery. Places within this place hold amazement and wonder.

Feeling calm and protected, you rest as if in a deep, sleeplike state . . . like a deep, deep sleep, yet with a feeling of mental alertness. You feel secure and peaceful, aware and focused.

Moving further and further in this journey
within . . . you hear the sound of the wind and
water rise and fall . . . then fade away. The storm
is still swirling and crashing . . . pounding and
flashing. Sometimes it seems near . . . other
times it seems far . . . far away.

But, in this place, you feel safe and secure . . .
calm and peaceful . . . distant and detached from
the fury of the storm that swirls around you.

You are unafraid, unbent, and unhurt . . . and
breathing in a way that is calm and relaxing . . .
calm and relaxing . . . feeling a special sense of
peace and security.

You awaken as if within a dream to a special
discovery . . . to the healing, soothing power of
warmth.

First, you feel the warmth around you . . . very
deep and complete . . . strong and thorough,
feeling the warmth deep within you, feeling its
soothing, healing power . . . calm and peaceful.

Then you notice that the storm has quieted. Less
and less raindrops are falling . . . less and less
water, swirling . . . less and less wind, blowing.

The warmth turns the water to steam . . . and
evaporates the raindrops . . . even before they
reach the ground. The sun comes out . . . and

shines its light through the rising steam. You
feel warm and soothed by the mist.

Take some time now to feel that special
feeling . . . that soothing feeling . . . calm and
comfortable . . . comfortable and relaxed.

Pause 10 to 20 seconds

Now you become aware of another healing
feeling . . . cool and refreshing . . . deep and
strong . . . numbing and soothing. You are now
barely aware of the storm.

Sensing cool and quiet . . . a faint swirling . . .
now soft and gentle . . . you see the cold
transforming the water of the storm . . . turning
it to snow.

Bright sparkling snow crystals float in the air
and reflect the light . . . then fall softly to the
ground. A blanket of quiet white . . . creates a
deep, deep restful sense of calm.

The whole landscape covered with snow . . .
looking soft and smooth . . . makes you feel
comfortable and relaxed . . . calm and at peace.

Pause 10 to 20 seconds

You will discover other places where you can
find a sense of calm and quiet . . . a sense of
soothing and healing.

Time is your friend and ally. Take the time you need to find a place of calm and quiet.

Pause for 1 minute

In a moment, you will prepare to leave your special place . . . But even as you think that thought you feel secure in your knowledge of this place that lies within.

Then you think about what you want to take with you . . . something that you found here that helped you feel calm and quiet . . . that gave you a sense of relief and rejuvenation . . . a sense of soothing and healing.

You know that when you journey back to this special place . . . you will find your way once again. You know that each time you come here . . . and then leave . . . you can take something with you . . . something that will help you find calm, rest, and relief.

But each journey will be different . . . You will recognize some familiar terrain . . . but still you will take a different path.

The more you journey to your special place . . . the easier it will be for you to find the way and the more secure and comfortable you will feel within this place. But most of all . . . after each journey you remain secure in your knowledge about this special place that lies within.

Pause

In a moment, I will ask you to take a deep breath and bring yourself back to the here and now.

Go ahead and take that deep breath now . . . and blow it out.

Come back to the here and now . . . with a calm, soothing, relaxing feeling. Keep that calm, soothing, relaxing feeling with you . . . as you open your eyes . . . and continue to rest comfortably.

Repeat the above instructions until everyone is alert.

Pond of Love

Julie T. Lusk

Time: 8 minutes

In this script, participants sit beside an imaginary pond that radiates love. Endless variations can be created by substituting different characteristics and virtues radiating from the pond. For instance, the pond may be full of peace, understanding, or forgiveness. You may also want to let the participants choose the characteristics on their own.

Be sure to use some type of relaxation exercise before going on to this script.

Script

Imagine that you are sitting beside a private, secluded pond. Nothing will disturb you. Look around the pond . . . take in your surroundings. What season is it? What colors do you see? Do you notice any smells? . . . Simply take in the scenery.

Now draw your attention to the pond . . . As you look at the pond, you realize that it is not an ordinary pond of water; it is a pond filled with love.

Feel love's energy radiating from the pond.

Feeling drawn toward the pond, see yourself coming closer to it . . . the pond that is radiating love. Look into the depths of the pond . . . It's full of love. See a beautiful mist hovering above the pond . . . Notice that the mist is made of love.

Breathe it in . . . It's fulfilling and satisfying. Each time you breathe in, feel the essence of love . . . surrounding and enfolding you . . . calming and satisfying you.

Breathing in, feel the love filtering in and entering your being. Smell it . . . feel it . . . bring the love into your being.

You notice a boat beside the pond . . . floating on the pond of love . . . sweet and pure love. See yourself approaching the boat. See yourself getting on board the boat . . . and floating on the pond of sweet and pure love . . . rocking gently back and forth, being fully supported by love.

Feel yourself reaching out toward the pond . . . the pond full of love. Splash the love upon you. Feel it soak into you . . . filling you with love. Allow it to enter the quiet center of your being . . . deep within you . . . in your own special center.

Your innermost center radiates with love.

Feel the love in your center growing . . .
expanding . . . throughout your entire body . . .
radiating out from your center . . . circulating
through and through.

There may be an area of your life . . . physical . . .
mental . . . emotional . . . spiritual . . . that could
benefit from being bathed in love. Feel the love go
to that area . . . bathing you . . . washing over
you . . . becoming a part of you. Feel the love.

Pause 15 seconds

If you wish, you may now send this loving
feeling to other people . . . to other places . . . to
other relationships.

Pause 10 seconds

Bring your attention back to sitting beside the
pond . . . feeling the love.

It is time to bring your attention back to
the present . . . Begin stretching and wiggling
whenever you are ready . . . and open your eyes.

Repeat the above instructions until everyone is alert.

Inner Smile

Lilias Folan

Time: 10 minutes

This gentle relaxation exercise has its roots in Zen meditation and will leave participants feeling inner harmony and happiness.

Script

Now slowly, slowly . . . knowingly . . .
place your body in a relaxing position . . . feet
well apart . . . arms away from your body . . .
back pressed against the surface on which it
rests, shoulders down—feel the space between
your shoulders and ears—chin down . . . nose,
chin, and breastbone in alignment.

Recall a time when you were upset or ill and
someone, maybe even a stranger, gave you a
big, genuine smile and suddenly you felt better.

The purpose of this exercise is to create a harmonious, happy condition within you. You can
practice the Inner Smile whenever you wish.
Use it at night as you relax in bed, to ease into
sleep, or use it to wake yourself up in the
morning. Share the Inner Smile with your
family . . . and friends.

You are lying in the familiar relaxation pose . . . your body is comfortable . . . spine supported. Let's go through a brief relaxation period, scanning the body . . . from your head . . . down through your body and to your feet . . . focusing on areas of tension . . . When you come across an area of tension, suggest it relax.

Pause

Feel the tension melt or soften . . . Begin stimulating that positive, smiling energy; not with a "make-nice" smile, but recall a memory that makes you feel good . . . perhaps of meeting someone you love and enjoy.

Pause

Let the corners of your mouth turn up . . . and continue generating this energy . . . as if you were touching a match to dry kindling. Feel it spreading happy, warm light . . . the smile softening the muscles around your mouth . . . warming your whole face.

Let the smile flow back into your mouth, releasing tension in your jaw muscle, then flowing over your tongue, to the tip of your tongue, your whole mouth filling with the warmth and light of the smile.

Again, stimulate the smile energy with an

appropriate memory. Then smile this energy up into your left eye, and then into your right eye.

Smile up into your left ear . . . and into your right ear . . . the warm, light-filled smile. Now, begin to smile down into the voice box . . . and swallow.

Smile the light into your physical heart . . . Send it warm, light-filled, loving thanks for circulating life throughout your body.

Smile the light of your smile into both lungs . . . Take your time . . . Resist moving on until you feel that smiling energy in each lung . . . smiling into the right lung and then into the left lung.

Now send that smiling light down to every organ beneath the abdomen wall—to your liver, spleen, kidneys, stomach, to the areas of digestion, elimination, reproduction.

Now smile into the large bones of your body . . . now into the small bones, into each vertebra of the spine. Then radiate the light of the Inner Smile throughout your whole body, filling all the curves and corners inside your body, each cell . . . Every cell dances with the energy of your Inner Smile

Pause

Radiate the smile through your whole

body . . . into your head, filling your good friend, the brain.

Shine illumination onto any emotional shadows in need of healing. In that light, fear and worry dissolve . . . forgiveness and insight grow and thrive.

Begin to expand that smiling light beyond the boundaries of your skin. Let it wave a cocoon of pure iridescent white light around you.

Lie here for a few minutes, surrounded by that cocoon of light. Only good can be here . . . only light . . . and love. Silently, affirm to yourself:

I release my day to the Light.

I release my past . . . any fears . . . negative thinking . . . the future . . . into the light.

I am a light being.

I radiate light throughout my body.

I radiate light to everything.

I radiate light to the planet earth.

I thank you, Higher Power, Holy Spirit, sacred Chi (thank whatever is comfortable for you). I thank you for everything, for everyone, and for me. Repeat that once again, with real meaning: I thank you for everything . . . for everyone . . . and for me.

Pause

And as we close, I send you my love and blessings. May the light of lights illuminate your every step . . . this day . . . and surround you with love and light as you drift off into sleep this night.

Repeat the above instructions until everyone is alert.

Taken from the audiotape program *Rest, Relax, and Sleep* by Lilias Folan. © 1991, Lilias Folan and Nityananda Institute. Published by Rudra Press, P.O. Box 1973, Cambridge, MA 02238. Used by permission.

Thoughts Library

Flora Kay

Time: 15 minutes

This script can help participants control wandering, stressful, distracting thoughts by having them exchange these thoughts for relaxing ones. Participants visualize putting away unwanted thoughts in a book with vinyl see-through pages and then opening up another imaginary book to experience a relaxing and beautiful ocean scene.

Be sure to use some type of relaxation exercise before going on to this script.

Script

Your entire body is relaxed to the best of your ability. Notice that you are breathing freely and easily . . . just breathing in . . . and out . . . in . . . and out.

As you relax further, turn your attention to your thoughts, take some time to get in touch with what is on your mind right now.

Just follow your thoughts and notice what is on your mind.

It is now time to practice taking control of your

thoughts. Doing so enables you to let go of unwanted, stressful thoughts, and to give yourself time to increase your concentration and your ability to remain focused and relaxed.

Imagine yourself going into your Thoughts Library . . . the place where you can let go of unwanted thoughts and take time for pleasant ones. Feel the peacefulness of the library . . . it is quiet, relaxed, and restful.

Take in a nice and easy breath and smell the aroma in this special library . . . Just breathe it in. Look around the shelves . . . see the different books. Do any titles stand out to you?

See or feel yourself moving toward a special section of the library where there is a selection of color-coded books stacked on brown shelves.

Looking closer now, you see that the books have smooth vinyl covers and are about the size of three-ring notebooks . . . Inside, they have vinyl pages filled with pictures that depict stories.

The books are color-coded . . . the ones with bright colors are for thoughts that have good feelings associated with them . . . the ones with dark and shadowy covers are for thoughts that worry you . . . that stress you.

Browsing through these valuable books gives
you the special ability to capture your thoughts
and to decide whether to save them for problem
solving . . . basket them . . . or store them for
another time.

See or feel yourself take down one of the dark
vinyl books . . . Hold it in your hands as you get
in touch with it. Feel or see yourself slowly
opening up the book of thoughts and pulling up
one of the see-through pages.

Carefully put every detail of a stressful and
worrisome thought or situation under the vinyl
see-through page. Close the book and put it
back on the shelf for a while. This will give you
time to realize whether the thought is worth
saving or not.

Let's take time now to look over the many
bright-colored books . . . the ones with good
feelings. Briefly leaf through the winter white
ones for ice-skating thoughts . . . the blue ones
for ocean sunrise and sunset thoughts . . . red
ones for rose garden thoughts . . . gold ones for
the flight of eagles . . . green ones for forests . . .
aqua for seashells . . . rainbow colors for the
many melodies of music . . . violet ones for
thoughts of friends . . . and orange ones for
thoughts of autumn.

You choose the blue ocean-sunrise-and-sunset
thought book . . . As you slowly open it, you feel
and see the sun rising slowly into the sky until it
bursts into bright sunshine . . . The sun feels
welcome and soothing . . . and has a clear white
light shining from it.

Turning to another page, you find a cool and
misty morning . . . The sky seems even more
blue than usual as it contrasts with the soft,
white puffy clouds.

See the clouds as they slowly move through the
sky. What do you imagine as you gaze at the
shapes of the clouds?

Below, the blue and green ocean waves are
peaked with white foam . . . ebbing and flowing
upon the sandy white beach.

The waves move in . . . and out . . . forming
patterns in the sand. The waves have a special
rhythm that comforts, relaxes, and soothes you.

You feel peaceful, calm, and serene. Feel the
water with your toes as you walk along the
water's edge. The sand is cool and moist under
your feet. The cool waves move back and forth
over your feet.

Leafing through the pages once again, you see

or feel yourself lying on a beautiful beach towel on the warm sandy beach.

Feel yourself absorbing the warmth of the radiant sunshine . . . feel the comfort of lying there firmly on the sand . . . feeling secure and safe as you let yourself sink comfortably down . . . feeling held . . . peaceful, calm, and serene . . . in harmony with the world around you . . . feeling at peace with your surroundings.

Turning to yet another page . . . you see yourself sitting in a red-and-white-striped beach chaise lounge, which feels as if it were made just for you.

As you calmly sit there, you meditate on the beauty of the scenery . . . absorbing the peacefulness around you . . . and feeling the peace deep within you.

It is your favorite kind of day. The afternoon slowly passes by as you relax on the beach . . . listening to the sounds of the ocean waves, the wind, and gulls.

You feel more and more relaxed as you listen to the ebb and flow of the ocean waves.

Soon the sun will begin to set and you know that it is time to return . . . The brilliant red and orange sun retreats below the ocean as it sets lower and lower and lower in the sky.

You feel so relaxed . . . and refreshed . . . and peaceful as you close the blue book . . . noticing the sound of the soft, mellow, gentle swish as you place it back on the shelf for another time of relaxation.

Pause

Begin to bring your attention back to this room . . . feeling rested and recuperated.

When you're ready, open your eyes, stretch out your arms and legs . . . and feel relaxed and at peace with yourself . . . Completely relaxed and at peace.

Repeat the above instructions until everyone is alert.

Personal Growth

Many people find it hard to make decisions, and many others find it difficult to make positive lifestyle changes. If this is true for you or your clients, try out these guided visualizations. Give your body and mind the chance to work *for* you instead of against you.

Read *Creative Visualization* and *Living in the Light* by Shakti Gawain for a description of the principles used in these scripts.

As always, be certain to use a relaxation script whenever advised to do so, and feel free to modify these scripts to fit your situation.

Visualizing Change

John Zach

Time: 10 minutes

In this script, participants spend time exploring and visualizing a desired behavioral change to enhance the change process.

Be sure to use some type of relaxation exercise before going on to this script.

Script

Allow yourself to enjoy a moment of relaxation . . . for there is no place you need to be for awhile.

Picture yourself preparing to step into either a warm shower or bath . . . The water temperature is perfect. Look at the steam coming off the water . . . and hear the water splashing against the sides of the shower or tub.

Now jump into that picture and feel yourself stepping into that warm, relaxing water . . . Allow the warm water to relax the different parts of your body even further.

Now imagine that you are floating to a room that has three televisions.

The first television shows you behaving in a way that is not helpful to you and that you would like to change . . . The second one shows you learning and behaving in a way in which you want to behave . . . and the third shows you in the future enjoying life in a different manner due to your new behavior.

Picture the first screen now. It shows a behavior that you would like to change.

After you acknowledge what behavior you would like to change, turn off this first screen.

Turn on the second set. It shows you learning and behaving in new and healthier ways.

Once you have learned enough about this behavior . . . turn off the second set and pay attention to the third one. It shows you in the future enjoying life in a different manner because of your new behavior.

As you see and hear this future movie, jump into the set and imagine being in this movie . . . feeling what it feels like to be successful in having changed yourself in a healthy and enjoyable way.

Now come out of the set and turn it off, then spend a minute back in the warmth and security of the warm water.

Pause

When you are ready, allow yourself to come back to the here and now, taking as much time as you like.

Then stretch out and open your eyes . . . feeling awake and refreshed as if you have slept a full eight hours.

Repeat the above instructions until everyone is alert.

Stop Smoking Relaxation Exercise

Jayne M. Schmitz

Time: 18 minutes

This script is intended to be used in conjunction with a smoking cessation program or a strategies for quitting program. It begins with a passive progressive muscle relaxation exercise to put participants at ease then offers positive suggestions on becoming smoke-free.

Script

Take a moment to get into a comfortable position either sitting or lying down . . . then close your eyes.

For the next few minutes I'd like you to listen to the sound of my voice . . . and as you listen, you may let your body begin to slow itself down nice and easy . . . Let all the stresses and strains of the day fade away.

You're beginning to relax . . . to let go . . . and to slow down. Let go of your body tensions right now as you listen with your mind.

131

A flow of relaxation makes its way from the top of your head, all the way down to the tips of your toes. You begin to relax as you feel your muscles letting go . . . They seem to melt.

Your breathing is natural and effortless. You're beginning to slow down . . . and let all the negative feelings fade away. You let the world fade away.

It feels good having relaxation move through your body . . . a wave of relaxation. And it begins at the very top of your head.

You allow your scalp to relax . . . and the relaxation flows downward across your forehead . . . through your eyebrows and eyes . . . down to your cheeks and nose . . . and across your mouth. You even let your jaw relax a little bit as you unclench your teeth.

You are practicing letting go of your body tension . . . It helps you to open your mind to your inner feelings and inner thoughts.

And as you listen you let go even more. Let the relaxation flow . . . Just imagine more and more relaxation flowing gently downward from your face and into your neck, causing all the muscles in your neck to let go . . . and relax. It's a slowing down that flows deep within you.

And just imagine this flow of relaxation spreading out across your shoulders . . . and down through your arms.

Relaxation flows through your upper arms . . . through your lower arms . . . and moves down into your hands, your fingers, and fingertips.

Imagine that all of the tight, tense feelings from your upper body are melting right out the tips of your fingers . . . Your upper body is letting go as you let the relaxation flow deeper and downward.

All tensions and all negative feelings fade away, and you relax even more through your chest and upper back . . . and down to your stomach.

You may even imagine that each time you take a breath in, you breathe in even more relaxation. And each time you breathe out, you let go of all tension. Just let all the negative feelings fade away as you continue to unwind and relax.

Imagine this wave of relaxation moving gently down into your lower back, and then to your hips . . . and thighs, which seem to melt . . . and you let it happen.

You feel the tensions leaving your body. You feel heavy and relaxed . . . your knees . . . your calves and ankles . . . and your feet . . . right down to the tips of your toes . . . feel heavy and relaxed.

And as you let your body get heavier and more relaxed, I'm going to count downward from 10 to 1 . . . and with each downward count allow your body to relax even more. 10, it's now time to relax . . . deeper at 9 . . . downward and deep at 8 . . . and you let go . . . limp and at ease . . . deeper at 7 . . . downward at 6 . . . deeper at 5 . . . and 4, just letting go . . . downward at 3 . . . deeper at 2 . . . and downward at 1 . . . feeling calm, safe, and comfortable.

Your eyes are closed, but your inner mind is open . . . and you're listening to all the suggestions, all the thoughts, and all the ideas that are going to help you reach your goal . . . to help you remain smoke-free . . . and to end your relationship with cigarettes. You choose to succeed.

This is *your* decision and *your* goal . . . so let your mind do the work now. Let your mind accept the positive feelings that come from being smoke-free.

You are in control now. *You* are able to control the urge to smoke . . . Your mind is strong, and anytime a desire or craving for a cigarette enters your mind, you'll cause that undesirable thought or feeling to fade away.

A technique to make this easier is by gently rubbing the thumb and first finger of one of

your hands together . . . Anytime and anywhere,
by simply rubbing your thumb and first finger,
and perhaps taking a nice, easy breath as you do
that, you allow the cravings to fade away . . .
and you realize you can handle the urge to
smoke . . . you can handle the feeling for a
cigarette.

Rub your thumb and first finger on one hand
together as you take a nice, easy breath . . .
Doing this now will help you remember this
relaxed feeling whenever you rub your fingers
together later . . . to help you control the urge
to smoke.

You have control now . . . and it feels so good to
be a nonsmoker. You've decided you want to be
healthier and you want to feel better . . . So relax
now . . . and let your mind be open to your
decision to change your life . . . your decision to
end your relationship with smoking.

Every day it will become easier and easier to be
that nonsmoker, and it will feel good to you . . .
you'll be proud to have the control. You've
brought yourself to a new level of control and
power by being able to talk on the phone . . .
drive your car . . . and be in all those situations
when it used to feel so right to light up.

You are succeeding now . . . making a change
that is very important to you . . . feeling positive

about what you are doing. Your choice to be smoke-free is a symbol for you that you want to improve your life.

You are choosing to be healthier . . . and you choose to do other things that enhance your health, like drinking lots of water . . . And the water tastes so good . . . and it's so refreshing, and it's washing the nicotine out of your body.

And you begin to exercise . . . gradually becoming more physically active . . . having more energy now. And you feel like you want to do all these things because you're now becoming a healthier person . . . and now you begin eating healthier foods, with lots of fruits and vegetables.

Your inner mind tells you again and again that you want to make it happen . . . Use your mind to drive the cravings away by rubbing your thumb and first finger . . . drinking lots of water . . . managing your weight . . . eating lots of fruits and vegetables . . . and exercising regularly.

All these ideas and feelings become a part of the new you . . . You begin to experience them every day of your life . . . You practice these new ways so that they become natural, real, and powerful for you.

You'd rather not smoke . . . and you can handle

any cravings now because they fade away and die. You have new outlets and new ways to handle your life . . . You've made the decision to remain smoke-free, and that feels right for you.

Pause

In a moment, I'm going to count to five and you will open your eyes. You'll feel awake and refreshed, and all the suggestions will work for you . . . Your decision to succeed and to be in control is very strong now . . . Your commitment to yourself is very strong now.

Now prepare to wake up . . . 1, you are becoming aware of your surroundings . . . 2, you are almost awake . . . 3, you feel alert . . . 4, you are awake now . . . and 5, you are wide awake and you open your eyes.

Repeat the above instructions until everyone is alert.

Imagery to Increase Basal Metabolic Rate (Learning Script)

Constance Kirk

Time: 12 minutes

This and the following imagery script focus on weight control by having participants imagine increasing their basal metabolic rates (BMR), which stands for the number of calories burned at rest.

Use this script until participants have mastered the visualizations, then have them switch to the shorter version that follows. It may be helpful to instruct participants on the location of the hypothalamus, pituitary gland, and thyroid gland. Advise them to make changes slowly and consistently instead of trying to make huge changes all at once.

To benefit the most from this or the shorter exercise, it is recommended that participants practice it twice a day for the first two weeks, then once a day for four weeks, and then just once a week.

A research project conducted at the University of Wisconsin, Oshkosh, showed remarkable results on the effectiveness of this script. For more information, contact the author at her address listed in the Contributors section.

Script

This imagery experience will help you relax and assist your body in doing something it already knows how to do . . . only better.

By using imagery, you can help your body burn food easier and faster . . . especially the food stored in your body as fat.

Relaxing will help you learn. It will help you focus on increasing your metabolism, which will allow you to burn more calories at rest than you usually do. Images will come to you easily and effortlessly. Merely relax and follow my voice.

Make sure you are warm enough. You cannot relax if you get cold during this activity.

Lie down or sit in a comfortable position. Stretch and wiggle around until you are comfortable.

Focus on your breathing . . . Feel the air going in and out through your air passages. Hear the air exchange. Feel the movement of your chest and stomach muscles as you breathe.

Pause 10 to 20 seconds

As you breathe out, imagine all tensions, worries, and discomforts leaving your body. Let go of everything you don't need or want.

Pause 10 to 20 seconds

As you inhale, breathe in life-giving force . . . pure, clean, energizing. Imagine the oxygen

139

bathing all the cells of your body, making them healthier and stronger.

Pause 10 to 20 seconds

This pure air dissolves all tension.

Pause 10 to 20 seconds

Feel the relaxation spread throughout your entire body.

Pause 10 to 20 seconds

Good. If you discover your mind drifting to other thoughts, don't worry about it. When you notice your thoughts drifting, bring your attention back to my voice. Follow my voice as effortlessly as a twig in a stream moves along with the current. Let go . . . Listen to the natural flow of the words and feel the natural flow of your body.

Now imagine the inside of your body and prepare to take an inner tour of your body . . . Your mind and body cooperate to allow you to travel anywhere in your body safely and easily. You are going on a sight-seeing tour, so just relax.

For the next minute, sit back and enjoy this trip through your imagination . . . Go along as you would on a leisurely sightseeing trip . . . even take a photograph of the things that impress you. Notice the location of stores of body fat.

Pause 1 minute

Good. It is natural and necessary for your body to transform food into energy even at rest. Your body is *continually* changing food into heat, which helps maintain or increase your body temperature.

And it continually changes food into mechanical energy necessary for your heart to beat, your lungs to breathe, your stomach to digest, and your muscles to move.

This transformation is not only safe and natural but is a process absolutely necessary for maintaining life.

Remember that this transformation, this burning of food, is continuous . . . it never stops . . . even at rest . . . even during sleep.

Body fat is a form of food storage. This fat is not stagnant but is constantly circulating. Therefore, it is available for your body to use as energy. Through the wonderful power of your imagination you are now going to increase your metabolism.

Let go and surrender to your imagination.
Don't worry about how *good* you are doing.
Remember that anybody can do this whether
they believe they can or not. It even works for
people who don't think they have a very good
imagination.

For the next minute, in any manner you wish,
imagine your body increasing its use of fuel.

Pause 1 minute

Good. As you know, there are specific
mechanisms built into your body which control
the rate of metabolism. Let's go to each of these
mechanisms to set the controls for a higher
metabolism.

First, in your imagination, go into your
hypothalamus to set your metabolic rate.
Ask permission to set the controls for a higher
metabolism. You do this by lowering the set
point. If there are no objections and you have
permission, change the controls.

Pause 5 seconds

If you have already traveled to the
hypothalamus and changed the controls, then
merely check the reading. Make adjustments if
necessary.

Pause 10 to 20 seconds

Before you leave the hypothalamus, thank it for allowing you to have control.

Pause

Now travel to the pituitary gland, which lies just below the hypothalamus. The more growth hormone circulating in the body, the higher the metabolism.

Visualize in your mind's eye the pituitary secreting more growth hormone . . . Remember that as an adult, growth hormone will not make you grow bigger unless you are weight training. Even then, the growth will be muscular.

Your mind is directing your body. Your body, because of its inherent wisdom, will only respond in safe and natural ways

Pause 15 seconds

Thank the pituitary gland for responding to your request.

Pause 5 seconds

Move along to the thyroid gland, located in the neck. Thyroxin and growth hormone both act to increase the number of calories burned in the body, which in turn produce more energy.

The more thyroxin circulating in the body, the higher the metabolism. Ask the thyroid to secrete more thyroxin . . . Visualize in any manner you wish, this increase in circulating thyroxin.

Pause 15 seconds

Thank your thyroid gland for responding to your request.

Pause 5 seconds

Now let's take a tour through the body again. Because you have increased the amounts of growth hormone and thyroxin and lowered the set point of your metabolic rate, you are presently burning more fuel . . . more fat. Your body's temperature has increased . . . Can you feel it?

Pause 5 to 10 seconds

This time, travel to any place you wish and imagine the production of energy, the burning of body fat . . . Let your imagination go and visualize this in any way.

Pause 30 seconds

Good. As you progress through your day, know that you have a naturally higher metabolism. At any time, resting or exercising, let your mind direct your body to adjust your set point and increase the levels of thyroxin and growth hormone and the rate of transformation of fuel to energy.

Your body continuously burns calories . . . now it does it faster, even at rest.

Pause

Now let your mind focus on the details of this room.

Stretch . . . and as soon as you are ready . . . gently open your eyes.

Repeat the above instructions until everyone is alert.

Imagery to Increase Basal Metabolic Rate (Shorter Script)

Constance Kirk

Time: 8 minutes

This script should be used after participants have gone through the preceding script several times.

Script

Lie down or sit in a comfortable position. Stretch and wiggle around a bit to get comfortable.

Relax with the thought that for the next few minutes you will devote your time to taking care of yourself. Images will come to you easily and effortlessly.

Now focus on your breathing. Feel the air going in and out through your air passages . . . Hear the air exchange. Feel the movement of your chest and stomach muscles as you breathe.

Pause 10 to 20 seconds

On the out-breath, let go of everything you don't need or want.

Pause 10 to 20 seconds

On the in-breath, take in the life-giving force . . .
pure, clean, energizing. Imagine oxygen bathing
all the cells of your body, making them healthier
and stronger.

Pause 10 to 20 seconds

Feel the relaxation spread throughout your
entire body.

Pause 10 seconds

When you notice your thoughts drifting away,
gently focus back on my voice.

Follow the suggestions effortlessly . . . go with
the natural flow of the words and the natural
flow of your body.

Now bring your attention to the inside of your
body . . . Notice that it is functioning better and
healthier than during your last visit.

Your arteries are cleaner, your blood flows more
freely, your immune system is stronger and
more efficient . . . you are burning fat faster . . .
you have more and bigger furnaces transforming stored food into energy. You burn body
fuel more naturally and easily.

Let go and surrender to your imagination. Don't worry about how *good* you are doing. For the next few moments, in any manner you wish, imagine your body increasing its use of fuel.

Pause 1 minute

Travel to the hypothalamus and check your set point . . . make an adjustment if needed.

Now travel to the pituitary gland. Visualize the pituitary secreting more growth hormone. Can you see it interact with the fat cells, the muscle cells?

Your inherent body wisdom will allow your body to respond in only safe and natural ways.

Move along to the thyroid gland in the neck and see it secrete more thyroxin. See the thyroxin acting to increase the number of calories burning in your body.

Take a tour through your body again. Because you have increased amounts of growth hormone and thyroxin, and have a lower set point, you are burning more fuel . . . more fat . . . and your body's temperature has increased.

Travel to any place you wish and imagine the production of energy, the burning of body fat.

Let your imagination go.

Pause 10 to 20 seconds

Be confident in your knowledge that you have a naturally higher metabolism. At any time, resting or exercising, let your mind adjust your body's set point, increase thyroxin and growth hormone, and burn more calories.

Your body continuously burns calories . . . now it does it faster, even at rest.

Pause

Let your mind focus on the details of the room. Stretch . . . and as soon as you are ready . . . gently open your eyes.

Repeat the above instructions until everyone is alert.

Peace for People Experiencing Grief

Belleruth Naparstek

Time: 25 minutes

This gentle and loving script helps people deal with their grief by guiding them to a special place full of beauty and healing energy. In this place, the grief and pain surrounding loss begins to be soothed and relieved.

Script

Get into a comfortable position . . . shift your weight and allow your body to be fully supported by your chair or bed or whatever is supporting you. Try to keep your head, neck, and spine straight.

Now take a couple of deep, full cleansing breaths . . . inhaling as fully as you comfortably can . . . deep into your belly if you can.

And as you breathe in . . . see if you can send the warm energy of the breath to any part of your body that's sore or tense or tight . . . and release the discomfort with the exhale . . . so you can feel your breath going to all the tight, tense places, loosening and softening them . . . and then gathering up all the tension and exhaling it . . . so that more and more, you are feeling safe

150

and comfortable, relaxed and easy, watching the cleansing action of the breath . . . with friendly but detached awareness.

And any unwelcome thoughts that come to mind, those too can be sent out with the breath . . . released with the exhale . . . so that for just a moment, your mind is empty . . . for just a split second, it is free and clear space, and you are blessed with stillness.

And any emotions that are rocking around in there, those too are noted and acknowledged and sent out with your breath . . . so that your emotional self is still and quiet, like a lake with no ripples.

And now, picture a place where you feel safe and peaceful and happy . . . a place either real or imaginary . . . a place from your past . . . or somewhere that you've always wanted to be. It doesn't matter . . . just so it's a place that feels good and safe and peaceful to you.

And allowing the place to become more real to you, in all its dimensions . . . look around you . . . take the place in with your eyes . . . enjoy the colors . . . the scenery . . . looking to your right . . . and to your left.

And feeling whatever you are sitting or standing on . . . whether it's sand . . . pine needles . . .

grass . . . a cozy armchair . . . or a nice, warm
rock in the sun.

And listening to the sounds of the place . . .
birds singing or leaves rustling . . . wind
or music . . . a crackling fire . . . or crashing
waves . . . just so your ears can become attuned
to the wonderful sounds of this place that is so
safe and peaceful to you.

You might feel a breeze blowing . . . crisp and
dry . . . or balmy and wet . . . or the warmth of a
cozy fire on your face and hands . . . Let your
skin enjoy the wonderful presence of this place.

And smell its rich fragrance . . . whether it's the
soft scent of flowers . . . or salt-sea air . . . sweet
meadow grass . . . or a forest floor covered with
pine needles..

And as you become more and more attuned
to the safety and beauty of this place . . . feeling
thankful and happy to be there . . . you begin
to feel a kind of tingling . . . a pleasant,
energizing something in the air all around
you . . . something that contains expectancy and
excitement . . . a sense that something wonderful
is just about to happen.

And you may even smile to yourself, because
perhaps you haven't had that feeling in a
while . . . but now you know with some

certainty that this place holds magic, and
something wonderful is about to happen.

And as that certainty settles around you, you
notice that the tingling is taking on a kind of
glow . . . that the air is alive with vibrant energy.

From somewhere above you a cone of powerful
white light softly and steadily moves down,
forming a vibrant tent of tingling energy all
around you . . . surrounding and protecting
you . . . illuminating everything it touches with
exquisite brightness . . . giving everything it
shines on a fresh, new beauty.

The air around you intensifies, glows, and
dances with sparkling energy . . . And with a
sense of gentle wonder for such stunning beauty,
you feel the tingling energy of the light moving
down into your body . . . softly entering your
head and neck . . . your shoulders . . . your chest.

Gently penetrating into the tightness around
your heart . . . slow and easy . . . massaging and
opening . . . steadily kneading and softening and
releasing the pain deep in your heart.

And continuing down the spine . . . filling your
back and torso . . . penetrating into the layers
of tissue, deeper and deeper . . . slowly and
steadily moving into every organ . . . cleansing
and clearing.

Sending a warm, vibrating softness into the
tightness in your belly . . . gently massaging
and opening . . . filling it with the powerful
reassuring softness of the light.

And moving down into your legs . . . filling your
feet . . . all the way to the tips of your toes.

Just let yourself feel the vibrant, healing energy
of the light, working its magic deep inside your
body . . . moving with deliberate intelligence
to the deepest places where pain is stored . . .
and feeling the spaces open up as you breathe
into them . . . fully and deeply . . . sensing the
beginnings of their opening and dissolving . . .
the beginnings of the heaviness starting to lift.

You come to realize you are not alone . . . that
you are aware of a warm presence all around
you . . . and looking around, surprised but not
surprised, you see that you are surrounded by
gentle, loving beings, immediately recognizable
as allies . . . smiling and nodding in the
remarkable light . . . warming you with their
protective presence.

One of them softly approaches you . . . and
with a wonderful, deep, gentle look, stares
directly into your eyes and gently touches
the center of your chest . . . with warmth and
softness . . . sending comfort right into the heavy
ache of your heart . . . soothing the torn, jagged

places . . . opening and warming and softening
all around the pain.

You can now breathe deeply, filling your whole
body with this generous, healing energy . . .
perhaps letting the tears begin to melt the armor
around your heart . . . as the eyes that gently
look at you nod and smile . . . showing you
that it is understood . . . how much hurting
you have done . . . it is understood, the stony-
cold aloneness you have felt . . . the wordless
ache of longing . . . the stinging regret . . . the
disappointment of interrupted dreams . . . the
pain, breathtakingly intense at one moment, and
heavy and dull the next . . . it is understood, all
the fear . . . the anger . . . the pain . . . all of it is
understood.

You feel the warmth begin to collect and radiate
through your entire chest, sending compassion
and forgiveness and reassurance to every corner
of your being . . . soft and easy . . . rich and
full . . . as you breathe into the opening spaces of
your heart . . . widened by the warmth of the
healing hand.

And suddenly you are certain . . . you know
with your whole heart, with your whole
being . . . that there is a place where nothing is
lost . . . where all the love and sweetness, direct
or disguised, that ever passed between you is
still alive . . . that all the love you have ever felt

for anyone at any time is alive and well in the
vast richness of your open heart . . . placed there
forever . . . rich and nourishing and boundless . . .
always available to sustain and nourish you . . .
whenever you need it.

Breathing in to touch it . . . breathing out to
let it move through you . . . feeling the body
soften and replenish . . . sending a gentle, healing
forgiveness all through you . . . a new compassion
for yourself . . . a different way of looking.

You understand that you are being shown . . .
that even this terrible pain might be a teacher . . .
showing you something you need to know . . .
about yourself . . . about who you are . . . who
you are becoming.

You understand that even this will look different
to you in time . . . when you know more about
who you have become . . . when you are
connected to your life in a new way . . . when
the pain has permanently softened . . . when this
has become part of the depth and richness of
the texture of your being.

You see in the deep, gentle warmth of the eyes
that look at you that it is understood that you
have seen this . . . that you have had a glimmer of
your own healing . . . that nothing has been lost to
the vastness of the heart . . . that the whole world
spins and thrives there . . . and so you can begin

to return to the peaceful stillness at your
center . . . breathing in the gentle soft
forgiveness that resides in the vast spaces
of your own open heart.

And as your gentle band of allies smile and
nod, your special one says to you, "Remember,
we are always here. It is you who come and go.
Call for us anytime and we will come."

And gathering up a handful of the glowing,
vibrating light, your ally places it in your heart
for safekeeping . . . your own special supply, to
use as needed.

And so, feeling peaceful and easy, you watch
as the light slowly begins to withdraw . . .
returning to wherever it came from . . . until it is
gone altogether . . . for now . . . knowing it is
yours to call forth again, whenever you wish.

And taking a deep, full breath, feeling the
widened spaces that are now opened, you once
again see yourself in your safe and peaceful
outdoor surroundings, feeling safe and easy . . .
although perhaps the colors around you are
brighter, the air more alive and fresh. You might
feel that something powerful has happened . . .
that a major shift has occurred . . . and will
continue to occur . . . with or without your
conscious working on it.

And you see very clearly that you can call forth this place, the powerful, healing cone of light, the special ones whenever you wish to further the work that you have already done.

Pause

And so, feeling yourself sitting in your chair or lying down, breathing in and out, very rhythmically and easily . . . gently and with soft eyes, come back into the room whenever your are ready . . . knowing in a deep place that you have done important healing work . . . that you are better for this . . . and so you are.

Repeat the above instructions until everyone is alert.

On Being a Wellness Professional

Tom Ferguson

Time: 15 minutes

This guided visualization helps participants discover a career path to follow that is in keeping with their inner talents and interests. Although it is written with a focus on professionals in the field of wellness, it can be adapted for almost any profession.

The purpose of this script is to encourage the development of an individualized niche as a wellness professional. To do this, it is important to really learn to listen to that quiet voice inside and to find the courage and the perseverance to develop your own style. It is vital to decide what's important for *you*. You must listen to yourself, for it is only by listening to your own inner voice that you can become authentic in your work in the wellness field. If you're not really responding to that inner voice, you're just playing a role.

To empower clients, we have to empower ourselves first. If we can't listen to our own quiet voice inside, if we can't connect with our own special passion, our own unique individuality, we're unlikely to be able to really listen to others. Playing a role, especially the authority role, gets in the way of real listening. Once we get stuck in the authority role, we become more concerned with some imposed version of doing it right than in really understanding the unique, one-of-a-kind person we're talking to. So it's a great aid to listening if we can each give ourselves permission to be our own unique person, which will then make it easier to let a client be a one-of-a-kind person, too.

Be sure to use some type of relaxation exercise before going on to this script.

Script

Please close your eyes and focus on your future career in wellness. Use your imagination . . . dare to be bold . . . dream big. What topic or vision of working in this area gets you most excited.

What would you really like to do in the wellness field that you're not doing now?

What kind of clients or patients or people are you most happy and excited to work with?

Is there an area of wellness that gets you so excited that you'd be happy to spend five or ten years becoming a world expert in it? If so, what is it? . . . It is all right to sense that it exists but not be quite sure what it is. Just open yourself up to the limitless potential and opportunities.

Pause

Okay . . . Now this one is secret. No one else is going to know. You don't have to share your answer with anybody . . . Is there an area of wellness that just bores the pants off you? That you'd be just as happy never to have to deal with again? A whole area that makes you feel sluggish and dull . . . as if you're trying to teach first graders about the four basic food groups?

Now ask yourself what it would be like to begin working in the area of wellness that you find most exciting and to gradually drop the areas you find most dull and boring . . . How might you go about doing this?

Pause

Suppose you were to define a unique approach to wellness that you could get really excited about . . . a whole angle that would be special and new and ideally suited for you . . . a niche that suits you so well that within a few years you might begin to develop a reputation as one of the world's experts on this topic. What would this approach be?

Let your imagination roam . . . discover . . . explore . . . have fun.

Pause

Bring your attention back to the present . . . and when ready, stretch and open your eyes.

Repeat the above instructions until everyone is alert, then go on to the follow-up section below.

Follow up

After you have identified a special niche, practice the following Clipping Exercise for the next thirty days. Read everything you can on your chosen topic(s). But do your reading with a scissors in hand or a copying machine nearby. Clip or copy any story or article that really grabs you. Put it away in a file. Read general newspapers, too, especially national newspapers like the *New York Times* and *USA Today*.

Meanwhile, keep on reading anything else that appeals to you, anything else you can get your hands on. Just remember, if it really grabs you, clip it or copy it. No matter what the topic. At the end of the month, open your file, spread out your clippings on your table or floor, and look for patterns.

Then do the Newsletter Exercise. Using all your favorite clippings, and writing up a simple, short introduction, if you wish, paste up a simple newsletter. Think of a title that reflects your main topic of interest or just pick a name that you like and put it at the top. List the best people, books, periodicals, ideas, and resources that relate to your chosen topic, and enclose any quotes you find especially interesting. The newsletter itself can be as simple and rough as you wish. Make copies of your newsletter and send them to the people you think would be most interested. See what kind of a response you get.

Contributors

Michael Arloski, Ph.D.
Arloski & Associates, 245 Redstone Drive, Bellvue, CO 80512. 970/484-3477. E-mail: info@realbalance.com www.realbalance.com.

Michael directs Real Balance Coaching and Training, offering personal and professional coaching, speaking, training, and seminars nationally and internationally. Michael's unique blend of Eastern and Western holistic stress management methods has been enthusiastically received in the United States and Thailand and at the National Wellness Conference. He is author of the *Stress Thrivers Relax Pack,* a two cassette relaxation/stress management training package. Michael is a past president of the Colorado College Counselors Association and the Ohio Society for Behavioral Health and Biofeedback.

James E. Borling, M.M., MT-BC, SAMI
Department of Music, Radford University, Radford, VA 24142. 540/831-5177.

Jim is the director of the Music Therapy Program at Radford University in Radford, Virginia. He received the title of fellow from the Association for Music and Imagery and makes use of Music Evoked Imagery in his private practice in Roanoke, Virginia.

Bob Fellows, M.T.S.
Mind Matters, Inc., P.O. Box 16557, Minneapolis, MN 55416. 612/925-2872.

Bob is a professional mentalist, illusionist, and educational consultant with a Master of Theological Studies from Harvard University. Fellows regularly gives presentations dealing with wellness and self-responsibility to students, educators, employees, executives, and national television audiences in the United States, Canada, and Australia. He is the author of *Easily Fooled: New Insights and Techniques for Resisting Manipulation.*

Tom Ferguson, M.D.
Self-Care Productions, 3805 Stevenson Ave., Austin, TX
78703. 512/472-1333. E-mail: DrTomHi@aol.com.

Tom is a self-care pioneer. He is president of Self-Care Productions and is a senior associate at Harvard Medical
School's Center for Clinical Computing. He founded the
influential journal *Medical Self-Care* and is medical editor
of the *Whole Earth Catalog.* In his book *Megatrends,* author
John Naisbitt cited his work as representing "the essence
of the shift from institutional help to self-help." Tom has
recently been involved in organizing the first series of con-
ferences in the United States on consumer health
informatics—the study and development of computer sys-
tems that support the informed, pro-active health consumer. His newest book is *Health Online: How to Find Health
Information, Support Forums, and Self-Help Communities in
Cyberspace* (Addison-Wesley, 1996).

Lilias Folan
c/o TSI Yoga, P.O. Box 43101, Cincinnati, OH 45243.

Lilias Folan introduced yoga to America on her long-
running PBS series *Lilias, Yoga & You.* She has written two
best-sellers and produced an award-winning yoga video
series entitled *Lilias! Alive with Yoga.* Call 1-800-321-4420
for information on her videos and other products.

Judy A. Fulop, M.S., N.D.
847/872-6218

Judy is Naturopathic Resident at Midwestern Regional
Medical Center and Cancer Treatment Centers of America.
She speaks and consults nationally and internationally on
guided imagery, psychoneuroiromunology, women's
health, and natural medicine. She was formerly the director of Well Life at Saint Joseph Health Center in Kansas
City, Missouri, where she integrated wellness within the
medical setting so that the community, patients, staff, and
physicians could benefit from wellness in the healing
process.

John Heil, D.A.
Lewis-Gale Clinic, 4910 Valley View Blvd., Roanoke, VA
24012. 540/265-1605.

John is a psychologist specializing in sport psychology and
behavioral medicine. He is coordinator of psychological
Services for Lewis-Gale Hospital Pain Management Center and provides sport psychology consultation to the
Commonwealth Games of Virginia, the United States Fenc-
ing Association, the Committee on Sports Equipment and
Facilities, and the Virginia Amateur Sports Association.

Flora Kay, R.N.
Interim Health Care, PO Box 2053., Roanoke, VA 24018.
540/989-0939.

Flora is especially interested in the areas of stress management, nutrition for stress, relaxation, and biofeedback for
chronic pain nursing. She has formerly worked in medi-
cal/ surgical pediatrics, home health nursing, and facilitated educational lectures and coordinated treatment for
chronic pain patients at the Lewis-Gale Pain Center .

Constance Kirk, Ed.D.
381 West Ann, Whitewater, WI 53190. 262/473-5761.

Connie is an associate professor in health education at the
University of Wisconsin-Whitewater. She has designed
programs to facilitate behavior change and conducts seminars in weight dynamics, using language for high level
performance and imagery for healing. She is the author of
*Taming the Diet Dragon: Using Language and Imagery for
Weight Control and Body Transformation.*

Julie T. Lusk, M.Ed, L.P.C., C.Y.I.
5678 Willnean Dr., Millford, OH 45150. E-mail:
JULusk@aol.com. www.relaxationstation.com

Julie T. Lusk, M.Ed., NCC, designs and implements internationally recognized mind/body and wellness programs for businesses, communities, medical centers, and

individuals. Her refreshing manner enables her to unravel mysterious concepts and present them in a useful and practical way as a speaker, teacher, writer and consultant. She enjoys sharing realistic methods to cope with stress, improve performance, and feel better emotionally, physically, spiritually, and mentally. Professionally, Julie has worked in health care management, higher education and community organizing. She has taught yoga since 1977 and is the creator of *Desktop Yoga*™.

Patricia A. McPartland, M.S., M.C.R.P., Ed.D., C.Ht., C.Ha. Southeastern Massachusetts Area Health Education Inc., P.O. Box 280, Marion, MA 02738. 508/748-0837

Patricia is an internationally known educator, writer, and lecturer and the executive director of SMAHEC, an organization that focuses on cross cultural competency training. She is certified in Holistic Aromatherapy and Hypnotherapy and is the author of *Promoting Health in the Workplace*. Patricia also conducts workshops on marketing, stress management, healing, aromatherapy, and maximizing your potential and is available for private consultation.

Belleruth Naparstek, LISW
c/o Image Paths, P.O. Box 5714, Cleveland, OH 44101. 800/800-8661.

Belleruth is a psychotherapist and the author of *Staying Well with Guided Imagery* (Warner Books), *Your Sixth Sense* (Harper San Francisco), and *Health Journeys,* twenty guided imagery tapes for people with specific health conditions. She regularly presents workshops on applying imagery to healing and personal growth.

Irene O'Boyle, M.A., CHES
Mid Michigan District Health Department, 617 North State Road, Suite A, Stanton, MI 48888. 517/831-5203. E-mail. 1662@nethawk.com.

Irene is the division director for health education in three rural counties in the middle of Michigan. She has worked in numerous health care settings, including college health services, doctors' offices, and hospitals. Irene enjoys all aspects of wellness, especially those with a prevention focus. She is the founder of the Gratiot County AIDS Resource Team, and in 1992 won the Gratiot County award for American Red Cross Volunteer of the Year. She is currently working on her Ph.D. in public health.

Jayne M. Schmitz, M.P.H.
617/832-7837

Jayne is Wellness Promotion Specialist at Blue Cross and Blue Shield of Massachusetts. She has five years of experience developing and implementing a corporate wellness program for an office park in Boston that holds over forty companies. She has always been interested in living healthfully and keeping fit She enjoys cycling, walking, gardening, and eating ice cream with her husband, Steve.

Elaine M. Sullivan, M.Ed. L.P.C.
Sullivan Associates, Inc., 2929 Marsann Lane, Farmers Branch, (Dallas) TX 75234. 972/243-5333.

Elaine is an international keynote speaker and consultant. She has presented workshops in the areas of wellness and human development to colleges and universities, hospitals, corporations, and community groups. She focuses on building healthy relationships, inner healing, the power of story, and the integration of mind/body/spirit. Her tape *Owning the Power of Your Story* can be ordered through Sullivan Associates, Inc.

Donald A. Tubesing, M.Div., Ph.D.
Whole Person Associates Inc., 210 West Michigan, Duluth, MN 55802-1908. 218/727-0500.

Don is a pioneer in the fields of stress management and wellness promotion. *Seeking Your Healthy Balance* and *Kicking Your Stress Habits* are his most popular books. Don's company, Whole Person Associates, publishes a wide variety of materials for trainers. Write or call for a free catalog.

167

Nancy Loving Tubesing, Ed.D.
Whole Person Associates Inc., 210 West Michigan, Duluth
MN 55802-1908. 218/727-0500.

Vice-president of Whole Person Associates, specialists in developing innovative stress and wellness resources for trainers and client corporations, Nancy created and edited the ten volume *Structured Exercises in Stress Management* and *Wellness Promotion* series. Coauthor of *Seeking Your Healthy Balance,* Nancy is also the soothing voice on many of Whole Person's unusual relaxation tapes.

John Zach, M.S.
University of Wisconsin-Stevens Point, Career Services, 134 Old Main, Stevens Point, WI 54481. 715/346-3226.

John is a career counselor / therapist in the Career Services Office at the University of Wisconsin-Stevens Point. Since 1975, John has provided training in the use of imagery in the areas of wellness, career development, and personal development.

Cross-Reference Index

The scripts from volumes 1 and 2 have been organized into the following categories to help you select the ones that are most appropriate for the issues you and your clients are working on. You'll find that certain scripts are listed under more than one category.

Behavior Change

Career Development

Centering

Enhancing Self-esteem

Especially for Children

Self-discovery/Developing Intuition

Shorties (less than 10 minutes)

Weight Management